ISBN 978-1-330-50604-2
PIBN 10071037

FB &c Ltd, Dalton House, 60 Windsor Avenue, London, SW19 2RR.
Company number 08720141. Registered in England and Wales.

For support please visit www.forgottenbooks.com

EXERCISES IN ENGLISH

SELECTED AND CLASSIFIED FOR CRITICISM OR CORRECTION

BY

H. I. STRANG, B.A.,

HEAD MASTER, GODERICH HIGH SCHOOL, ONTARIO.

REVISED, WITH ADDITIONS, BY

G. R. CARPENTER,

ASSOCIATE PROFESSOR OF ENGLISH IN THE MASSACHUSETTS INSTITUTE OF TECHNOLOGY, AND NON-RESIDENT LECTURER ON RHETORIC AND ENGLISH COMPOSITION AT WELLESLEY COLLEGE.

BOSTON, U.S.A.:
D. C. HEATH & CO., PUBLISHERS.
1894.

Printed by C. H. Heintzemann, Boston, U. S. A.

INTRODUCTORY NOTE.

MY attention was first called to this book by the mere mention of its title in the *Academy*. Having long been in search of a good book of the kind for myself, and for many other teachers who had consulted me, I procured a copy; and the result was that I at once urged upon my friends, *Messrs. D. C. Heath & Co.*, its republication in this country, with a confident assurance that it would furnish a valuable aid in the teaching of English just where such aid is most needed, — that is, in the practical test and application of those rules of right usage which are *taught so much too much*, yet so little verified and applied, in the habitual school-teaching. Being thus in a certain sense responsible for the book, I could not deny the duty of saying a word in its behalf; yet the author's own preface is so clear and so sufficient, with regard to its purpose and its right use, that he has left nothing for me to say. Teachers who will examine it will not, I think, need the assurance of the preface to the fifth edition, that it is fitted for wide usefulness in many schools. Indeed, one of its chief recommendations is that it is adapted to use with *any* English grammar, or *without* any at all; and that, within quite an extensive range of skilfully shaped exercises, suited for different grades, it appeals always to the intelligent judgment, without reference to any given rule. If this word from me, who have now for many years felt the want of just such a help for myself and for others, should contribute to secure even the examination of this little book, I should feel I had done, vicariously, a real service to what I regard as in itself the most difficult, and in its results usually the most unsatisfactory, branch of school work.

EDWARD S. JOYNES.

SOUTH CAROLINA COLLEGE,
March, 1888.

AUTHOR'S PREFACE.

In laying before my fellow-teachers this collection of Exercises in English, for Criticism and Correction, it may not be amiss for me to say a few words in regard to its origin and its object.

I had not been long engaged in high-school work before I discovered that in many cases pupils who had a ready command of grammatical rules and definitions, and who were fairly proficient in analysis and parsing, were, yet, seemingly unable to detect common and undoubted errors in sentences in every-day use. Further experience showed me that even after they had learned to notice and correct mistakes in sentences given them for that purpose, many of them would continue to make the same or similar mistakes in their ordinary speaking and writing. I was led to conclude, therefore, that, accustomed as the majority of our pupils are from childhood to hearing incorrect forms of speech used by those around them, special and systematic drill is necessary to teach them to notice and guard against these wrong forms; and that this drill should be oral as well as written, in order that both the ear and the eye may be enlisted in the cause of good English, and trained to assist the student.

Holding this opinion, and not finding in any of our text-books a suitable collection of exercises for such drill, I began to compile one; and this book is the result of my labors. Whether other teachers have felt the same want, and whether, if so, this collection will meet it, is for them to say. I hardly expect that it will prove wholly isfactory to any one; but, nevertheless, I have been encourag believe that it will be found sufficiently comprehensive and pr to be of some service. It is not intended to take the place other book, nor has it been prepared to suit any particular w Grammar or Composition. My plan has been to give under each ing examples of all the common, typical errors of that class, and by frequent review exercises to accustom the student to be on his g at all points. I have inserted, also, a few sets of questions bearing directly on the correct use of different forms of expression. While, however, I have endeavored to include examples of all common errors, I need scarcely say that teachers may find it necessary to drill particularly and repeatedly on certain points, and for that purpose may have to supplement the exercises I have given; and that in some localities it may also be necessary to add a few dialectic or provincial forms of expression. In fact, any teacher who will take the trouble to note down, from day to day, words and sentences which he hears or sees in his school work, can make for himself a better collection of examples for oral drill than any book can furnish him.

A few of the examples have been selected from text-books and examination papers; a few more have been kindly contributed by friends or pupils; the rest have been gathered at intervals from a great variety of sources. As my object is to call attention to the mistakes, and not to the persons who have made them, I have not thought it either necessary or wise to give any references; and should any one, on looking through the book, find that he has been an unintentional contributor to its pages, I trust he will not take offence, but rather be glad that his mistakes are being put to so good a use. I have not spared my own blunders, and have, therefore, felt less hesitation in availing myself of those of others.

In conclusion I wish to say that I shall be glad to receive any criticisms or suggestions, in order that the next edition may be made more useful.

H. I. S.

Goderich, Ontario,
August, 1883.

EDITOR'S PREFACE.

At almost all the New England colleges the requirement in English is now literally uniform. At each college the examination consists of two parts — the writing of a short composition on a subject taken from one of a given list of books, and the correction of certain specimens of bad English. "The candidate will be required to write," says the catalogue of the Massachusetts Institute of Technology, for instance, "a short English composition — correct in spelling, punctuation, grammar, idiom, and division into paragraphs, and plain and natural in style — on some subject already familiar to him. He will be judged by how well he writes, not by how much he writes. For convenience, and in order that the candidate may be acquainted with good models of style, the subjects will be taken from one or more" of certain standard books, with all of which the applicant is expected to be familiar. "The candidate will also be required to correct specimens of bad English set for him at the time of the examination." The principles which underlie these requirements are, it seems to me, these: first, that a boy of sixteen or seventeen, properly fitted for college or for a technical school, should be able to write correctly and with some ease on subjects which he already knows; second, that he should know what is right and what is wrong in matters of grammar, syntax, and the like, about which there can be no possible doubt. These two principles, it will be noticed, are respectively the bases of the two parts of the admission examination. Let us consider them separately.

The first point is one which our preparatory schools sometimes wil-fully, sometimes carelessly, neglect. Were it possible, [illegible] of English would, I think, prefer that there should be n[illegible] sion examination in English, and that the candidate sh[illegible] by the English of all his examination papers, not by t[illegible] single paper. Such a system is perhaps not practica[illegible] but we should bear in mind that the object of this part [illegible]

tion in English is not to satisfy ourselves that the candidate possesses a given amount of information, but simply to make sure that he is sufficiently fluent and correct in expression to enable him to carry on his work in other branches, as well as in English, with profit to himself and without hindering others. For in college and in technical school alike the general complaint of the various departments of study is that many students are unable to express themselves satisfactorily. Such students come to us spelling badly, without any proper sense of English idiom, writing awkwardly and with great effort. They are obviously, in short, as unfitted for many parts of their college or professional training as they are for that written communication with private individuals or public bodies which, to a greater or less degree, must form a constant part of every man's professional or private life. Such men, then, come to us heavily handicapped in our common struggle for expression; and it is to the preparatory schools that we look for such methods and results of teaching as shall reduce to a minimum this percentage — already too large — of students who may perhaps be able to think, but have no adequate means of showing us by written words that they think or what they think.

The principle which underlies the other part of our examination that of correcting specimens of bad English — is a simple one. Here we test not expression, but knowledge. Rhetoric really consists of questions of taste and questions of absolute right and wrong. Drill in matters of taste we can afford to leave, for the most part, until the student is a freshman in college. There he can best attain skill in the exact choice of words with all their finer shades of meaning, in deftly framing them into well-balanced sentences, in coherent logical structure both of paragraphs and of the larger units of composition, in all that sound and nice thinking out into language which makes a man write clearly, forcibly, and pleasantly. But there is much in writing which is not a matter of taste, but of knowledge. And that knowledge a candidate should have when he presents himself for the admission examination. He should spell correctly, he should be familiar with the main principles of punctuation, he should know the difference between *shall* and *will* and *lie* and *lay*, and, in general, he should be exactly informed about plain questions of syntax and idiom about which there can be no doubt. That an average candidate does not have this exact knowledge the reader will find by examining the following random ·tracts from the essays written at an admission examination:

"On the shoar of the Arcadian land, the small village of Grand-Pré was siduated: . . . here, too, her farther lived and worked on his fertil farm; at peace with his neighbors, with all the world."

"In preparing for the Institute this fall, I was only studying my 'conditions,' of two years ago, when I was told I would have to take all of the examinations over, and the result will be, that I will be 'conditioned' in six, and perhaps seven studies."

"In the grave yard in Philadelphia, there lies to nameless graves side by side."

If boys will write in this fashion, the examiner must find some means of testing their knowledge point-blank. This he does by printing a dozen sentences or so, in each of which there are palpable errors, and asking the candidate to correct them. If he cannot detect common blunders when they are so isolated as to provoke discovery, it is not likely that he will be successful in expelling the same errors when they occur — *currente calamo* — in his own composition.

For the purpose of preparing candidates for this second part of the examination Mr. Strang's "Exercises" has proved especially valuable. Experience has shown, however, that the book needed a further revision which should adapt it more particularly to the use of teachers fitting pupils for the examinations for admission to our colleges — a use for which the book was not originally intended. Mr. Strang, unfortunately, has not been able to find leisure for this task, but it is with his full consent, and to some extent in accordance with his advice, that I have undertaken it.

The changes I have made are largely of two kinds, suggested in each case by the character of a large number of examination books written by pupils drilled on Mr. Strang's book in its original form, and by the work done in their freshman year by candidates similarly trained. First, I have inserted, wherever it was possible, such references to good text-books as would state clearly the principles on which corrections of the faults specified should be based, for I believe that in most cases the teacher will get better results by using these *exercises* in connection with a text-book which shall lay stress on the *principles* involved. For the same reason I have added, in the form of footnotes, authoritative statements from various sources on questions of doubtful usage, or on other points in regard to which explicit information might not be easily accessible to the pupil. Second, I have in some instances taken out errors which current and reputable colloquial or written use accepts as idiomatic. As I have said above, this part of the examination tests only the pupil's knowledge of English grammar, English idiom, and his general common-sense in matters of language. I have also inserted a number of exercises on punctuation, and added such typical examination papers as will show the teacher and the pupil precisely what the task is which they are undertaking.

Before beginning this book, the pupil should have had a thorough training in Whitney's "Essentials of English Grammar," or in Whitney and Lockwood's "English Grammar," or in some text-book equally good, if such can be found. Williams's "Composition and Rhetoric" and Meiklejohn's "English Grammar" may be used in connection with these exercises. Better than these is "Longmans' School Composition." Preferable even to this in many ways is Professor A. S. Hill's "The Foundations of Rhetoric," which unfortunately appeared just too late for me to insert references to it at the heads of the exercises. The book is so well arranged, however, and so well indexed, that neither teacher nor pupil will find any difficulty in turning directly to what he wishes.

Two statements more in conclusion. First, the teacher must not forget that this homœopathic device of producing good English by the use of bad is open to great and real dangers. Pupils may sometimes need but very little drill of this sort: more would impress on their memories wrong forms or unidiomatic constructions rather than proper forms and idiomatic constructions. Rarely will the pupil need to go through the entire book. The teacher's judgment must tell him where to stop, but he will be guided by remembering that such drill must always be subordinated to that of actual composition. The pupil must be taught not only to know bad English when he sees it, but to write good English. Second, all who are concerned in this little book, the author, the publishers, the editor, — and the editor in particular, — will be very glad to receive from teachers or from pupils who use the book any corrections or suggestions that may lead to adapting it still further to the specific purposes for which it is intended.

G. R. CARPENTER.

MASSACHUSETTS INSTITUTE OF TECHNOLOGY,
BOSTON, MASS., December 12, 1892.

REFERENCE BOOKS.

Every well-furnished school library should include the Century Dictionary, the latest edition of Webster or Worcester, Stormonth, Skeat's Etymological Dictionary, Murray's A New English Dictionary, and Smith's Synonyms Discriminated.

The following books deal, to a greater or less extent, with common errors in speech or writing or with English grammar. In most cases they may be consulted with profit by the pupil as well as the teacher.

Ayres's The Verbalist (D. Appleton & Co.).
Hill's The Principles of Rhetoric (Harper and Brothers).
Hill's The Foundations of Rhetoric (Harper and Brothers).
Hodgson's Errors in the Use of English (D. Appleton & Co.).
McElroy's The Structure of English Prose (Armstrong & Son).
Salmon's Longmans' School Composition (Longmans, Green, & Co.).
Bain's Higher English Grammar (Longmans, Green, & Co.).
Earle's English Prose (G. P. Putnam's Sons).
Morris's Historical Outlines of English Accidence (Macmillan & Co.).
Whitney's Essentials of English Grammar (Ginn & Co.).
Whitney and Lockwood's English Grammar (Ginn & Co.).

On the principles of Rhetoric the teacher should consult Wendell's English Composition (Charles Scribner's Sons). For the history of the English usage in regard to particular words see the Century Dictionary, The New English Dictionary, and Dr. F. Hall's Modern English, his Recent Exemplifications of False Philology, and the letters by him that appear from time to time in the New York *Nation*.

TABLE OF CONTENTS.

Part I.

ACCIDENCE.

Part II.

SYNTAX.

PART III.

SPELLING AND PUNCTUATION.

PART IV.

STYLE.

PART V.

PART I.

INFLECTION.

NOUNS.

I. — WRONG PLURAL FORMS.
II. — WRONG POSSESSIVE FORMS.

References: Whitney, sections 121–138; Morris, sections 77–94, 97–101; Bigelow, pp. 75, 37; Meiklejohn, sections 17–29. There are so few possible errors in the formation of plurals and possessives — the only existing noun-inflections in English — that the pupil should learn once for all to avoid them. Besides correcting the sentences given below, he should also answer the questions which follow them. Where his knowledge fails him, he can readily find the information he needs in the books referred to above or in any trustworthy dictionary. Before beginning another exercise, the teacher should be sure that the pupil understands thoroughly the few principles here involved.

EXERCISE I.

1. Take two cupsful of flour, and one of sugar.
2. He accounted for all monies received by him.
3. There are three Mary's in the class.
4. Eight Henries have sat on the throne of England.
5. I think that her two son-in-laws might support her.
6. He generally forgets to cross his ts or dot his is.
7. You can scarcely tell her 5s from her 3s.
8. Court-martials were held at various points to try the captured insurgents.
9. How many cantoes have you read?
10. Such crisises may occur in the history of any enterprise.

11. Summons were issued for the chief offenders.
12. These specimens belong to different genuses.
13. The animalculae in water can be seen quite plainly with it.
14. Many an early geological strata is thus clearly visible.
15. We have opened several cases of mens' and boys' overalls.
16. Look at the trains of these ladie's dresses.
17. Six month's interest was due on the note.
18. Ten days notice requires to be given in such cases.
19. I saw a sign with "Boat's to hire" on it.
20. For goodness sake don't let him know about it.
21. Virgils similies are mostly borrowed from Homer.

QUESTIONS.

1. What is the plural of: bamboo, cameo, canto, echo, embryo, folio, grotto, hero, potato, octavo, piano, two?[1]
2. What is the plural of: colloquy, valley, Henry?[2]
3. What is the plural of: aide-de-camp, animalculum, analysis, appendix, bandit, beau, chef d'œuvre, cherub, crisis, datum, focus, formula, genus, genius, hypothesis, index, larva, memorandum, minutia, phenomenon, seraph, stigma?
4. What is the plural of: German, Mussulman, talisman?

---

[1] "If the singular ends in *o* preceded by another vowel, the plural is formed regularly by adding *s*. If the singular ends with *o* preceded by a consonant, the plural is generally formed by adding *es*. Proper names ending in *o*, and the following common nouns, together with a few others from the Italian or Spanish hardly Anglicized, form the plural regularly:—

albino	duodecimo	junto	octavo	quarto	solo
canto	fresco	lasso	piano	rotundo	stiletto
cento	grotto	limbo	proviso	salvo	torso
domino	halo	memento	portico	sirocco	tyro."

Bigelow's *Handbook of Punctuation*.

[2] "Nouns ending in *y* preceded by a consonant or by *qu* form the plural by changing *y* into *ies*. But if the *y* is preceded by a vowel, *s* only is added for the plural. Some proper names ending in *y*, simply add *s* for the plural; as, *Henry, Henrys; Tully, Tullys*."—*Ibid.*

5. What is the plural of: cannon, fish, gallows, heathen, trout, summons?
6. What is the plural of: attorney-general, court-martial, charlotte russe, knight-templar, man-servant, major-general?
7. What is the possessive case of: lady, ladies, princess,[1] princesses?

ADJECTIVES.

Errors in the use of

I.—The So-Called Articles, *an*, *a*, and *the*.
II.—The Demonstratives, *These* and *Those*.
III.—Comparative and Superlative Forms.

References: Whitney, sections 219–221, 197–202; Morris, sections 108–110; Meiklejohn, pp. 29, 32, 33.

EXERCISE II.

1. What sort of a house does he live in?[2]
2. Such a man does not deserve the name of a gentleman.
3. There must have been more than an hundred of them.[3]
4. Is he an African or an European?
5. The government is a (an?) hereditary monarchy.
6. A lion is the emblem of England.
7. She is entitled to the third of the property.

---

[1] "A noun of more than one syllable ending in an *s* or *z*-sound sometimes omits the possessive sound, in order to avoid the disagreeable repetition of hissing letters. In such a case, the apostrophe is written alone at the end of the word."—Whitney's *Essentials of English Grammar*.

[2] Here the indefinite article is quite unnecessary.

[3] "The present rule is to use *an* before a vowel-sound (including *h* mute, as *an hour*); *a* before a consonant-sound (including *h* sounded, and *eu-*, *u-* with sound of *yū-*, as *a host*, *a one*, *a eunuch*, *a unit*). But in unaccented syllables, many, perhaps most, writers still retain *an* before sounded *h*, some even before *eu*, *u*,—as, *an historian*, *an euphonic vowel*, *an united appeal*,—though this is all but obsolete in speech, and in writing *a* becomes increasingly common in this position."—Murray's *A New English Dictionary*.

8. It describes the life of a young man and woman who were forced to leave their homes when Acadia fell into the hands of the English.[1]
9. The old and new opinions had their active partisans within the walls of the college.
10. I don't like these sort of pens.[2]
11. It isn't safe to trust those kind of people.
12. No man ever had a faithfuller friend.[3]
13. There could not have been less than fifty people in the room.
14. I have nothing farther to say to you at present.[4]
15. The last news is that they are to start on Monday.
16. Give this book to the youngest of the two girls.
17. He answered better than any boy in his class.
18. London has the largest population of any city in the world.
19. The S. has the largest circulation of any other paper in the county.

---

1 "Errors are not unfrequently made by omitting to repeat the article in a sentence. It should always be repeated when a noun or an adjective referring to a distinct thing is introduced; take, for example, the sentence, 'He has a black and white horse.' If two horses are meant, it is clear that it should be, 'He has a black and a white horse.'"—Ayres's *The Verbalist.*

2 "*Kind of* (also *sort of*) runs into certain marked idioms. It is used with a following noun to express something like or resembling or pretty near to what the noun expresses; as, he is a *kind of* fool (that is, not far from being a fool). Then, in careless and vulgar speech, it is transferred (especially in the abbreviated form *kind o'*, pronounced kind ǫ, and often written *kinder*, where the *r* is never pronounced) to use before an adjective; as, that is *kind o'* good; he acted *kinder* ugly: and even before a verb; as, he *kind o'* (*kinder*) laughed. Also in phrases like 'what *kind of* a thing is this?' 'he is a poor *kind of* fellow,' *kind of* has come to seem like an adjective element before the noun; and hence before a plural noun, after words like *some*, *all*, and especially *these* and *those*, it sometimes keeps the singular form; as, *these kind of people*. This inaccuracy is very old, and still far from rare, both in speaking and in writing; but good usage condemns it."—*The Century Dictionary.*

3 *More* and *most* may be used before any adjective or adverb which admits of comparison, and are generally used with words of more than two syllables with which the use of the suffix *-er* or *-est* would be awkward. Euphony is the sole test in doubtful cases.

4 *Farther* is generally used only when relative distance is implied.

20. We started off one evening with a kind father and aunt as chaperones.
21. You of all other girls in the class ought to be the last to complain.

PRONOUNS.

Wrong Forms or Wrong Use of Personal, Adjective, and Relative Pronouns.

References: Whitney, sections 149 ff.; Morris, chapter XII.; Meiklejohn, pp. 22–28.

EXERCISE III.

1. Aren't you afraid of his cutting hisself?
2. They ran away and hid theirselves.
3. This is a later edition than your's.
4. Our's is much larger than their's.
5. Pick up them books off the floor.
6. Mr. M. and myself took a walk down to the bank.[1]
7. He has several editions, either of which will serve your purpose.
8. Neither of the three methods is absolutely correct.
9. There is a row of elms on either side of the road.[2]

---

[1] "*Myself* is properly used in the nominative case only where increased emphasis is aimed at.

'I had as lief not be as live to be
In awe of such a thing as I myself.'

'I will do it *myself*, I saw it *myself*.' It is, therefore, incorrect to say, 'Mrs. Brown and myself were both very much pleased.'" — Ayres's *The Verbalist*.

[2] "In Old English and early Middle English *either* appears only in its original sense, 'each of two,' or as an adverb equivalent to 'both'; but about the beginning of the fourteenth century it assumed the disjunctive sense, 'one or the other of two.' This disjunctive sense has so far prevailed that in modern English such expressions as *on either side* = 'on both sides' are felt to be somewhat archaic, and must often be avoided on account of their ambiguity." — Murray's *A New English Dictionary*.

10. These two boys are always quarrelling with one another.
11. The scholars soon get acquainted with each other.[1]
12. He walked up and down from one end of the room to another.
13. I don't know whether Tom and myself have enjoyed anything more.
14. He went about the room, from one to the other, seeking sympathy.
15. I trusted to my horse, who knew the way better than I did.[2]
16. Even newspapers who advertise them are liable to be fined.
17. He is the greatest poet which this century has produced.
18. He remembered the names of most of the authors of which we had been speaking.
19. It will take all which he has earned this week.[3]
20. He was the first scholar who succeeded in answering it.

---

[1] "*Each other:* now generally used when two persons or things are concerned, but also used more loosely like *one another.*" — *The Century Dictionary.*

"A distinction is set up in the schools between *each other* and *one another;* and yet scarcely a good author can be found who does not use the two forms interchangeably." — A. S. Hill, *Our English*, p. 33.

[2] "In modern use *who* and *whom* are applied regularly to persons, frequently to animals, and sometimes even to inanimate things when represented with some of the attributes of humanity, as in personification or vivid description." — *The Century Dictionary.*

[3] "Some teachers insist that the relative *that* should be used, instead of *who* or *which*, when the relative clause serves to restrict the meaning of the antecedent, and that *who* or *which* should be used, instead of *that*, when the relative clause adds something to the meaning of the antecedent or explains it; and yet the best authorities, from Addison to Anthony Trollope, obey no such rule, but are guided by the ear in their choice between *who* or *which* and *that.*" — A. S. Hill, *Our English*, p. 33.

"*Who*, *which*, and *that* agree in being relatives, and are more or less interchangeable as such; but *who* is used chiefly of persons (though also often of the higher animals), *which* almost only of animals and things (in old English also of persons), and *that* indifferently of either, except after a preposition, where only *who* or *which* can stand. Some recent authorities teach that only *that* should be used when the relative clause is limiting or defining: as, the man *that* runs fastest wins the race; but *who* or *which* when it is descriptive or coördinating: as, this man, *who* ran fastest, won the race; but though present usage is perhaps tending in the direction of such a distinction, it neither has been nor is a rule of English speech, nor is it likely to become one, especially on account of the impossibility

21. I gave it to the boy what brings the milk.
22. A short time ago a letter appeared in your paper from myself.
23. It's appearance in this country surprises me.

EXERCISE IV. — REVIEW.

1. Don't buy any more of those sort of pencils.
2. Apply to Messrs. C and D., Barristers and Attornies.
3. These are the only cities who have adopted the system.
4. He brought three hats, neither of which was mine.
5. What kind of a bird is that on the fence?
6. Did you ever read Bunyans Pilgrims Progress?
7. Which is the heaviest, her's or mine?
8. Where did you get them apples?
9. It was the cowardliest act I ever heard of.
10. They keep coming in two's and three's.
11. It's name we decided on before we had seen it.
12. Of all other places in the world it's the last that I should think of.
13. You can't tell his ns from his us.
14. It presented an unique appearance.

---

of setting *that* after a preposition; for to turn all relative clauses into the form 'the house *that* Jack lived *in*' (instead of 'the house *in which* Jack lived') would be intolerable. In good punctuation the defining relative is distinguished (as in the examples above), by never taking a comma before it, whether it be *who* or *which* or *that*. Wherever *that* could be properly used, but only there, the relative may be, and very often is, omitted altogether: thus, the house Jack built or lived in; the man (or the purpose) he built it for. The adjective clause introduced by a relative may qualify a noun in any way in which an adjective or adjective phrase, either attributive or appositional, can qualify it, and has sometimes a pregnant implication of one or another kind: as, why punish this man, *who* is innocent? *i.e.*, seeing, or although, he is innocent (= this innocent man). But a relative is also not rarely made use of to add a coördinate statement, being equivalent to *and* with a following pronoun: as, I studied geometry, *which* I found difficult (*and* [I] found *it* difficult); I met a friend, *who* kindly showed me the way (*and he* kindly, etc.). This way of employing the relative is by some regarded as a Latinism, and condemned; it is restricted to *who* and *which*." — *The Century Dictionary*, under *who*.

15. One of the negroes sang two soloes at the concert.
16. You never saw a wretcheder looking specimen of humanity.
17. Prove your answer by casting out the 9s.
18. She is a better writer than any scholar in her class.
19. He showed me several, but I did not care for either of them.
20. He sets the hardest papers of any examiner I know.
21. He has tried without success the old and new method of cure.
22. He would talk no farther with us.
23. I gave it to one of the men which were working in the yard.
24. I heard that one of his brother-in-laws had bought the farm.
25. We kept them as mementoes of our six weeks holiday trip.
26. Wanted, a nurse and housemaid [two servants].
27. He must have fired not less than five or six shots at it.
28. I met Mrs. C. and himself on their way to church.
29. She doesn't like these kind of pianoes.
30. Many an one would refuse to do it.

VERBS.

I.—The Use of the Wrong Auxiliary.
II.—Wrong Forms for the Past Tense and the Past Participle.
III.—Using Transitive Verbs for Intransitive Verbs.

References: For most of the errors in the following exercise it will be sufficient for the student to consult a dictionary when he is in doubt. If he needs additional information about the principles of conjugation, he will be likely to find it in Whitney, chapter VIII. The teacher should assure himself that the pupil thoroughly understands the distinction between *sit, sat, sat; lie, lay, lain,* etc., and *set, set, set; lay, laid, laid,* etc. The distinction between *shall* and *will* is less simple, but not less important. See Whitney, sections 282–286.

EXERCISE V.

1. Can I have the use of your ruler for a little while?
2. They wanted to know if they could not have a holiday.

3. Will I find you at home this evening?
4. Would I be allowed to try the examination?
5. I hope we will be in time to get good seats.
6. He was afraid that we would miss the train.
7. I have resolved that I shall make the attempt.
8. He had little hope that they should accept the offer.
9. I knew he done it, for I seen him do it.
10. You have went over that lesson several times.
11. He must have forgot to put the cork in the bottle.
12. He came very near getting his leg broke.[1]
13. He rung the bell twice this morning.
14. The children sung several hymns.[2]
15. They sunk several wells in the neighborhood.
16. The toast was drank with great enthusiasm.
17. Hc must surely have mistook the house.
18. I think that you might have wrote and told us.
19. You might have chose something more appropriate.
20. He would have froze to death if we had left him.
21. The lesson is tore out of my book.
22. He throwed it over the fence and run for home.
23. He jumped in and swum across.

---

[1] "Of the past participle, ***broken*** is still the regular form, but from the end of the fourteenth century this was often shortened to ***broke***, which was exceedingly common in prose and speech during the seventeeth and eighteenth centuries, and is still recognized in verse." — Murray's *A New English Dictionary*.

[2] "A class of verbs form their present, preterit, and participle thus:

" *sing, sang, sung; begin, began, begun.*

"Such are *ring, sling, spring, swim*, and *stink*; further, *drink, shrink, sink*, which have for participles also *drunken, shrunken, sunken* (though these are now used chiefly as adjectives). All these verbs, however, sometimes form their preterit like the participle, as *sung, swum, sunk*. Of *spin*, the old preterit *span* instead of *spun* is now out of use, and we say only —

" *spin, spun, spun.*

"And the same is the case with *cling, fling, sting, string, swing, wring, slink*, and *win* (*won*).

In *run, ran, run*, the present is like the participle." — Whitney, *Essentials of English Grammar*, p. 113.

24. It will be all eat up before you get there.[1]
25. He had began his sermon before they entered.
26. He must have ran all the way home.
27. The passengers all beseeched him to return.
28. He said that his feet swole up to a great size.
29. Stung by her reproaches, he went and hung himself.[2]
30. The river had overflown its banks during the night.
31. After he laid down he remembered he had left it laying on the table.
32. You had better go and lay down for a little while.
33. She could not get her bread to raise properly.
34. I wish you would set still while I am copying this.
35. He was forced to fly the country in consequence.
36. He plead (pled) earnestly to be allowed to try.
37. You may have trod on it without noticing.[1]
38. I hope that he has beat them all this time.[1]
39. Didn't you know that he had forbade us to go there?
40. Two fatal errors underlaid his theory.
41. The town was burned, the cattle and goods stolen, and the people carried to a distant land.
42. The scene of Evangeline was lain in a small town in Nova Scotia.
43. A little child crept in at his half-open door, lied down on the hearth, and went to sleep.

EXERCISE VI.—REVIEW.

1. Which is the farthest north, New York or San Francisco?
2. I would like to hear his opinion of those sort of desks.

---

[1] Consult the *Century Dictionary* or the *New English Dictionary* for confirmation of this correct but nearly obsolete past participle.

[2] The verb *hang* represents two originally distinct verbs in older English; hence the double forms of the preterit and past participle. To signify a mode of capital punishment "*hanged* is still used both as preterit and as past participle, especially in legal phraseology."—*The Century Dictionary.*

3. I seen it laying on your desk a few minutes ago.
4. What sort of a proposition is it?
5. The tug rescued two vessels, who were in distress.
6. It is likely that I will be gone before you return.
7. He must have drank nearly three spoonsful of it.
8. They asked if they could not go out at recess.
9. Several combatants had already fallen on either side.
10. Surely he can't have ate it all already.
11. He don't seem to show much sense.
12. It claims to have the ablest staff of any of its contemporaries.
13. Can't we go when we finish this sum?
14. We have come to the conclusion that we will not be able to accept his offer.
15. He looks as if he had laid there all night.
16. An elephant don't usually like a rhinoceros.
17. It was decided that Mr. A. would accompany them to the city.
18. See if he don't turn out to be a failure.
19. Will we do this one the same way we done the last?
20. It is the likeliest place of all others in town to find him.
21. I was in hopes that we would have a chance to see him.
22. Tom has a better memory than any boy I know of.
23. If I had not broke your stick you would never have run home or began to cry.
24. The same man which left the parcel took it away again.
25. He found that the water had raised several inches.
26. He went about from one door to the other begging.
27. It was the peacefullest meeting they had had for some time.
28. He would have went this morning if I hadn't forgot to waken him.
29. It is two stories higher than their's.
30. For him through hostile camps I wend my way
For him thus prostrate at thy feet I lay.

ADVERBS.

THE USE OF ADJECTIVES FOR ADVERBS AND ADVERBS FOR ADJECTIVES.

References: The general differences in form and in use between the adverb and the adjective can be easily found in any good grammar by the student not familiar with them. There are cases, however, over which he will have to think carefully. Certain words are, and always have been, used indifferently as adverbs or adjectives. We certainly say *walk fast*, *speak loud*, *speak low*, *come, quick*; but there are comparatively few words of this sort. For the use of adverbs or adjectives with neuter verbs, see Whitney, section 354.

EXERCISE VII.

1. He behaved so bad that I had to suspend him.
2. She seemed real glad to see us.
3. He acted very different from his brother.
4. He writes plainer than he once did.
5. Walk as quiet as you can.
6. I managed that part of it easy enough.
7. He acted as friendly as if there had never been any quarrel.
8. The children marched quietly and orderly through the hall.
9. He acted very independent about the matter.
10. He scattered the seed quite thick on the ground.[1]
11. He spoke quite decided on that point.
12. The room smelt strong of tobacco.[1]
13. She went to bed and slept sound till morning.[1]
14. They were exceeding glad to see him.[1]
15. Isn't it near finished yet?
16. He ought to dress more suitable to his position.
17. Just as like as not you will meet him on the road.[2]
18. No one else could have looked so finely.
19. They acted very unfriendly towards us.
20. How sweetly these roses smell!

---

[1] Consult a dictionary on this point.

[2] *Like*, as an adverb, for *likely* is a common colloquialism and not without authority (see Othello, iii. 4), but in print it is unusual and archaic.

21. How beautifully your garden looks this morning!
22. The order must have sounded harshly to them.
23. He did it easier than I expected.
24. The stick he used was about that long.[1]
25. He was illy equipped for the journey.
26. He was very displeased about it.[2]
27. He was too injured to be taken home.
28. In my then circumstances the note was of no use to me.[1]

PREPOSITIONS.

The Use of the Wrong Preposition.

The pupil should trust to his sense of idiom in correcting the following sentences. Where that fails him he should consult a dictionary. In some cases a verb or a phrase may be followed by either of two prepositions, sometimes with a difference in meaning, sometimes without. The pupil should notice carefully the following instances.

Compare to or *compare with.*

"Two things are *compared* in order to note the points of resemblance and difference between them; they are *contrasted* in order to note the points of difference. When one thing is *compared to* another, it is to show that the first is like the second, as in Luke xv. the sinner is *compared to* a lost sheep, etc.; when one thing is *compared with* another, it is to show either difference or similarity, especially difference: as, the treatment of the Indians by Penn may be *compared with* the treatment of them by other colonists of America. *Compare* and *contrast* imply equality in the things examined; *compare to* and *compare with* do not, the object of the verb being the principal subject of thought.

'*Compare* our faces, and be judge yourself.'

—Shakespeare, *King John*, i. 1.

---

[1] Consult a dictionary on this point.

[2] "The adverb *very* is the singular and undivided property of the adjective,—*e.g.* 'very tall, very wise, very good,'—but it will not go with a verb. And this is the rationale of that rule which is laid down about the qualification of participles, viz. that *very* is not to be joined with a participle. We do sometimes hear 'very pleased,' but 'much pleased' is more correct."—Earle's *English Prose*, p. 53. But cf. Dr. F. Hall in the *Nation*, Oct. 13, 1892.

'Goethe *compared* translators *to* carriers, who convey good wine to market, though it gets unaccountably watered by the way.'—T. W. Higginson, *Oldport*, p. 202.

'*Compare* dead happiness *with* living woe;
Think that thy babes were fairer than they were,
And he that slew them fouler than he is.'
Shakespeare, *Richard III.*, iv. 4.

'All this luxury of worship has nowhere such value as in the chapels of monasteries, where one finds it *contrasted with* the ascetic ménage of the worshippers.'—H. James, Jr., *Trans. Sketches*, p. 306."

—*The Century Dictionary.*

Differ from or *differ with.*

Differ. "1. To be unlike, dissimilar, distinct, or various in nature, condition, form, or qualities: used absolutely or with *from:* as, the two things *differ* greatly; men *differ from* brutes; a statue *differs from* a picture; wisdom *differs from* cunning.

2. To disagree; be of a contrary opinion; dissent; be at variance; vary in opinion or action: used absolutely or with *from* or *with:* as, they *differ* in their methods; he *differs from* other writers on the subject.

'If the honorable gentleman *differs with* me on that subject, I *differ* as heartily *with* him.'—Canning.

'The first thing that tests a boy's courage is to dare to *differ from* his father.' W. Phillips, *Speeches*, p. 247.

'They agree as to the object of existence; they *differ* as to the method of reaching it.'—J. F. Clarke, *Ten Great Religions*, i. 4."

—*The Century Dictionary.*

Different from or *different to.*

"When in the predicate, *different* is either used absolutely: as, the two things are very *different;* or followed by *from:* as, the two things are very *different from* each other; he is very *different from* his brother. But the relation of opposition is often lost in that of mere comparison, leading to the use of *to* instead of *from.* This use is regarded as colloquial or incorrect, and is generally avoided by careful writers.

'*Different to* is, essentially, an English colloquialism; and, like many colloquialisms, it evinces how much stronger the instinct of euphony is than the instinct of scientific analogy.'—F. Hall, *Modern English*, p. 83.

'An amazement which was very *different to* that look of sentimental wonder.' Thackeray, *Vanity Fair*, p. 182."

The Century Dictionary.

EXERCISE VIII.

1. Divide these apples between these three boys.
2. I found it very different to what I expected.
3. Compare your work to his, and you will see the difference.

4. It seemed quite grand in comparison to mine.
5. He let his axe fall in the creek, while crossing.
6. The accident is likely to be attended by serious consequences.
7. She seemed quite overcome by sorrow at the discovery.
8. Is the music accompanied by the words?
9. He was accused with acting unfairly as judge.
10. He was quite ill with typhoid fever at the time.[1]
11. Try to rid yourself from all prejudices.
12. I hope that he will profit from his experience.
13. I beg to differ from the last speaker.
14. I did it in compliance to their request.
15. It flew up in the tree before I was ready to fire.
16. The whole room was redolent with the perfume.
17. He refused to conform with the regulations.
18. I did not take notice to what he said.
19. He was rather noted for his fondness of fast horses.
20. She felt the need for some one to advise her.
21. How do you reconcile this statement to your previous one?
22. She had not been accustomed with such treatment.
23. There was too long an interval between each game.
24. I wish to divide it in three equal parts.
25. Just contrast this picture to that.
26. I cannot entirely acquit him from blame.

CONJUNCTIONS.

I. — Conjunctions Wrongly Used.
II. — Words Wrongly Used as Conjunctions.

The chief errors in this exercise are the following. The student should be on the watch for them. (1) *Different than* for *different from; do not know as* for *do not know that; doubt but what* for *doubt* [*but*] *that; like* for *as; scarcely . . . than* for *scarcely . . . when; without* for *unless.* Another important error, frequently

[1] Is not this idiomatic English? — Editor.

illustrated in this exercise and succeeding exercises, is that by which a clause beginning with *and* or *but* and a relative (*i.e. and who, but who, and which, but which,* etc.) is used without being preceded by a corresponding relative clause. For instance, we may say, "I have an old book, *printed* at Antwerp in 1540 *and* once *owned* by Adam Smith"; or "I have an old book *which* was printed at Antwerp in 1540 *and which* was once owned by Adam Smith"; but *not*, "I have an old book, *printed* in Antwerp in 1540 *and which* was once owned by Adam Smith." The student should not let this point go by without understanding it thoroughly, for the error occurs with great frequency in careless writing. There are instances, however, in which a preceding participial or adjectival clause is so plainly equivalent to a relative clause that no one hesitates to use *and who, and which,* or whatever the collocation may be, in a position where it would not be, by strict logic, justifiable; but such cases are not common.

EXERCISE IX.

1. I don't know as I can give you his exact words.
2. It could not have got away without somebody untied the halter.
3. Scarcely had he gone to bed than there came a knock at the door.
4. Hardly had he left the room than the prisoner attempted to escape.
5. No sooner had he opened the door when the flames burst forth.
6. Directly he reached home he sent for the doctor.[1]
7. I will start at it immediately they have gone.
8. He took quite a different view than I did.
9. I prefer to wait a few days than to accept an inferior article.
10. Who could do otherwise but accept such an offer.
11. Why don't he walk like me?
12. He seemed very different than he used to.
13. Why don't you do like I do?
14. It treated him just like a cat treats a mouse.
15. There is no doubt but what he said so.
16. He gave her a handsome pony, and which cost him fifty pounds.
17. They captured several prisoners but whom they treated very fairly.

[1] An error much more common in England than in the United States.

18. He found that after paying all expenses that there would be a small sum left.
19. The chances are ten to one but he will forget it.
20. Neither the foreman or his assistant had seen it.
21. Stand on the desk so as all can see you.
22. Lord Evensdale did not live long after his rival returned, he was murdered by an old enemy, but which Henry Morton quickly avenged.[1]
23. Fifteen years before we find Silas living in a house by the side of a stonepit, in the town of Rarelow, he had a friend in his native village and of whose friendship he thought much.
24. The Marquis of Lafayette Webster also addressed with much feeling and relates how this gallant young man gave up so much in order that he might aid a people weak and oppressed, and who desired to fling off a tyrant's yoke.
25. He paid a great tribute to the name and fame of Lafayette, one of the first leaders of Republicanism in France and who had come once more to the country now free and united and which he had helped so nobly to defend.

EXERCISE X.—REVIEW.

1. He must have come after we had went home.
2. How will we know which of the two is best?
3. She was disgusted at him for acting so silly.
4. I cannot explain all the minutia of the process.
5. Their farm lays in a different direction to ours.
6. Your method seems quite simple compared to his.
7. He claims to have answered the most questions of any boy in the class.
8. It seems that he acted wiser than they thought.
9. He fell in the river and was nearly drowned.
10. You will scarcely find a more universal blunder.

---

[1] In this sentence and the next notice an error in structure. See Exercise XXXIV.

11. She told them to set up straight so as she could see them all.
12. To their great astonishment they discovered there several stratas of coal.
13. What is the distance between each telegraph pole?
14. He chose this verse because he thought it would be the easiest learned.
15. After a few minutes search they found it laying in a corner.
16. He died very sudden, I am told.
17. He acted just like a boy does when he is telling a lie.
18. I have no doubt but what we will all be benefited by it.
19. Of all other vices covetousness enters deepest into the soul.
20. No other course was left them but to accept his resignation, and which they accordingly did.
21. Mamma, can't we have a party on Saturday?
22. I think you acted very foolish in refusing it.
23. Will I go? It don't look like rain now.
24. It ended in establishing his authority firmer than ever.
25. I will be ten years old next Monday.
26. There is scarcely any one so poor but what can give something.
27. It wasn't Tom that done it, for I seen his hat lying in the hall.
28. The book is illustrated by several fine engravings.
29. He would not go without I promised to pay his expenses.
30. The case is different with city battalions, who are composed mainly of intelligent mechanics and artisans.
31. It was certainly a most remarkable phenomena.
32. He said that he had often swam across it.
33. It must be some sort of a beetle, I think.
34. He said he didn't know as it would be of any use.
35. The roof and the walls had given way and fell in.
36. Will I be allowed to choose either of the three?
37. Neither he or his sister knew anything about it.
38. The name was spelled different than usual.
39. I wouldn't be surprised to hear of his failure.
40. He had forgot to lock the door before he laid down.

41. Who is that girl setting near the window?
42. There was not the slightest need for so much waste.
43. She was that faint she could hardly walk.
44. Her's was the neatest done of all that I saw.
45. He did all that laid in his power to help us.
46. The bell began to ring directly we left the house.
47. They were scholars of a very different type to Bentley.
48. How sadly she must have felt at parting from them.
49. It had been arranged that he would be chairman.
50. I didn't know but what you might have forgot.

EXERCISE XI. — REVIEW.

I. — *Which of the italicized words in the following sentences is preferable? Why?*

1. It tastes quite *strong* (*strongly*) of cloves.
2. He told them to sit *quiet* (*quietly*) in their seats.
3. I fear that he will pay *dear* (*dearly*) for his rashness.
4. They lived just as *happy* (*happily*) as before.
5. This carriage rides *easy* (*easily*).
6. He felt very *bad* (*badly*) at being beaten.
7. Your piano sounds quite *different* (*differently*) from ours.
8. He stood *firm* (*firmly*) in his place.
9. The *latest* (*last*) report. He lives *farther* (*further*) away.
10. *This* (*these*) molasses. *This* (*these*) news.
11. It looked *strange* (*strangely*) to see him in your place.
12. He brought me a ten-*foot* (-*feet*) pole.
13. He must have *drank* (*drunk*) several *spoonfuls* (*spoonsful*).
14. It sounds *bad* (*badly*) to hear you say that.
15. They made sixty runs in their first *inning* (*innings*).

II. — *Distinguish between* —

1. My sister's photograph. A photograph of my sister (sister's).
2. The tailor and clothier. The tailor and the clothier.

3. Half a dollar. A half dollar.
4. I found the way easy (easily).
5. It looks good (well).
6. She looks sad (sadly).
7. He looked quiet (quietly).
8. (A) few know of it.
9. She was the greatest actor (actress) of her day.
10. She has done her sum. She has her sum done.
11. He (has) deposited the money in the bank.
12. He felt sore (sorely).
13. A red and (a) white cow.
14. Have you no other than (but) this?
15. He gave the child a few pennies (a few pence).
16. The third and (the) last volume.
17. The box came safe (safely).
18. The stage starts (will start) at six o'clock.
19. He was telling us about an (the) adventure he had.
20. The (a) lion is emblematic of courage.

III. — *Construct sentences illustrating the correct use of the following:* —

1. Angry at, with.
2. Compare to, with.
3. Consist of, in.
4. Die of, by.
5. Differ from, with.
6. Divide between, among.
7. Familiar to, with.
8. Live in, at.
9. Overcome by, with.
10. Reconcile to, with.
11. Taste of, for.
12. Content with, in.
13. Concur with, in.
14. Overwhelmed by, with.
15. Agree with, upon, to, in among.
16. Call at, on, for.
17. Copy from, after.
18. Enter into, upon.
19. Impatient with, at, of, for, under.
20. Inquire of, into, for, about, after.
21. Intrust to, with.
22. Killed by, with.
23. Wait on, for.

IV. — (*a*) *Distinguish in meaning.*

1. You will (shall) know the result to-morrow.
2. I will (shall) not be the only one to suffer.
3. Will (shall) he be allowed to withdraw it?
4. Will (shall) there be any charge for admission?
5. He thought she would (should) have another chance.
6. I shall (will) be the first to sign it.
7. He thought he would (should) go.
8. Do you think I would (should) take it?
9. He states that he will (shall) not attend.
10. If you did that you would (should) be punished.

(*b*) *Which of the italicized forms in the following should be used? Why?*

11. *Will* (*shall*) you be sorry to leave Toronto?
12. He tells me that he *will* (*shall*) be ten next month.
13. *Will* (*shall*) I be allowed another trial?
14. He has decided that he *will* (*shall*) not return it.
15. He offers a prize to whoever *will* (*shall*) guess it.
16. We *would* (*should*) be pleased to have you call and see it.
17. *Would* (*should*) you be surprised to hear of it?
18. I *would* (*should*) write to him if I knew his address?
19. What *would* (*should*) we do without you?
20. He promised that it *would* (*should*) not occur again.
21. I did that lest he *would* (*should*) suspect my object.
22. It is requested that no one *will* (*shall*) leave the room.
23. I *would* (*should*) much prefer to go by the boat.
24. They have agreed that the race *will* (*shall*) be rowed again.
25. If he *would* (*should*) fail to come I *would* (*should*) have to go.

(*c*) *Fill the blanks correctly with* SHALL *or* WILL, *or* WOULD *or* SHOULD.

26. —— we have time to call for it?
27. —— there be time to call for it?

28. I —— go and nobody —— prevent me.
29. I —— feel greatly obliged if you —— tell me.
30. If you —— call for me I —— be glad to go with you.
31. He did better than I —— have done.
32. I dare say that if you —— ask him he —— give it to you.
33. Though I —— die for it yet —— I not deny it.
34. —— candidates be allowed to use instruments in drawing the figures?
35. I —— be sorry to see him plucked.

PART II.

SYNTAX.

CONCORD OR AGREEMENT.

I. — WANT OF AGREEMENT BETWEEN THE VERB AND ITS SUBJECT.

References: Williams's *Composition and Rhetoric*, Lesson XIII., p. 49; Longmans's *School Composition*, sections 66–74. Teachers using other text-books can readily give their pupils notice of the corresponding sections, if such references are needed for the proper understanding of the principles underlying the following exercise.

EXERCISE XII.

1. Each of the candidates were allowed another trial.
2. Not one of all those boys were able to answer the question.
3. Nearly every one of the applicants were from this county.
4. Neither of the answers given to it were quite correct.
5. Have either of you seen my pencil?
6. Neither the mayor nor the sheriff were at the meeting.
7. Either ignorance or carelessness have caused this.
8. Nobody but the speakers and the reporters were allowed on the platform.
9. Nothing but trials and disappointments seem to await me.
10. Economy, as well as industry, are necessary to achieve such a result.
11. The costliness of his arms and apparel were evident at a glance.
12. Efficiency, and not numbers, are what we should aim at.
13. Every door and every window were crowded with spectators.

14. A fine collection of apples were particularly noticeable.
15. Pharaoh, with his whole army, were drowned in the Red Sea.
16. More than one accident has happened in that way.[1]
17. Was you at school the day it happened?
18. It is one of the hardest papers that has ever been given.
19. It may have been one of the men that works in the foundry.
20. To this cause, no doubt, is due most of the failures.
21. What is the mood and tense of the following verbs?
22. Sufficient data has been given to solve it.
23. Thou art the man that hast done this great wrong.
24. I am a man that have seen something of the world.
25. He don't look like a man of that sort.

II.—The Subject or the Predicate Pronoun in the Wrong Case.

References: Williams, Lesson XII., 1–4, 7, 9; Longmans, sections 75–77.

EXERCISE XIII.

1. Her and I are in the same class at school.
2. Henry and him soon began to quarrel.
3. They don't succeed any better than us.
4. She is older than me, but I am nearly as tall as her.
5. It seems that they, as well as us, had mistaken the house.
6. He said that you and me might go if we liked.
7. I gave it to a man whom I thought was the proprietor.
8. Give it to whomsoever seems to need it most.
9. It must have been her that you saw, not me.
10. It wasn't him that gave it to me.
11. It couldn't have been them that we passed.
12. It may have been us that you heard.
13. I should never have imagined it to be he.
14. Whom does he think it could have been?
15. Who do you take me to be?

---

[1] Is this not idiomatic English?—EDITOR.

III. — Appositives in the Wrong Case.

IV. — Pronouns not Agreeing with their Antecedents.

References: Williams, p. 46, sections 1–6; Longmans, sections 236, 237.

EXERCISE XIV.

1. Jones, him that won the prize for drawing, has gone to Montreal.
2. Give this book to young Smith, he that is sitting by the window.
3. Not a boy in the class knew their lessons to-day.
4. Each of the gentlemen present offered their assistance.
5. Neither of the workmen had brought their tools.
6. Neither the chairman nor the secretary would give their consent.
7. The father as well as the son agreed to use their influence.
8. Nobody but a fool would have left their money in such a place.
9. Nearly every one of those present promised their support.
10. Either Mr. A. or Mr. B. will, I have no doubt, lend you their copy.
11. Any pupil wishing to dispose of their copy will find a purchaser.
12. If any one wants it let them say so.
13. Whoever has a grain of class spirit in them should use their influence in raising the necessary funds.
14. He isn't one of those men that would abandon his principles for office.
15. I must confess that I am a man that can't keep my temper in such cases.

EXERCISE XV. — REVIEW.

1. Which of you boys left your books laying on the desk?
2. I thought he acted rather strange this morning.
3. One after another rose and expressed their approval.
4. Who do you think he took her to be?

5. I like it the best of any machine I have seen.
6. How could any person get such an idea into their head?
7. Can I have it after you are done with it?
8. There was lots of fun at the meeting last night.
9. The oldest of the two is about as tall as me.
10. Neither of the sisters were at church this morning.
11. She, with a few friends, procure a boat and float down the river.
12. In 1886 I went to one of the public schools in Brooklyn, where grammar and English was studied in connection with other subjects.
13. Your own conscience, and not other men's opinions, are to be your guide.
14. Perhaps it wasn't her that you saw.
15. It must belong to one of the prisoners which escaped from the jail yesterday.
16. He seemed to think that any sort of an excuse would do.
17. I will not be surprised to find that there was more than one in the plot.
18. It is thought to have been him that first suggested it.
19. It is one of the best answers that has yet been given to the question.
20. Nearly every one of the exercises she gave me had mistakes in them.
21. No city in Canada has suffered so much from fires as Quebec.
22. Of that large collection there remains but a few imperfect specimens.
23. We will all be anxious to learn the result.
24. He could not account for all the phenomena that was witnessed.
25. Whom did you say it was that gave it to you?
26. It seems that Mary and her went to school together.
27. I read it slow enough for any one to follow me.
28. The man whom we thought was him proved to be an entire stranger.

29. The moral is that perseverance, coupled with patience and prudence, are sufficient to achieve such results.
30. It is one of the words that doubles the *l* before another syllable.
31. A large part of the exports consist of spices.
32. Not one in ten of them are likely to pass.
33. I don't know as I will have any farther need for it.
34. Hardly had he resumed the chair than the trouble began again.
35. One after another rose and offered their services.
36. I didn't know but what it might be some sort of a trap.
37. Neither he or Irving have accomplished such results as Kean.
38. The opinions expressed are the writer's own and for which no one else is responsible.
39. More than one case has occurred where an innocent man has been hung.
40. We the undersigned has made up our mind to try the entrance examination at July.

V. — Wrong Tenses or Moods.

References: Williams, Lesson XIV., p. 52; Longmans, sections 290–295, 308–311, 316–319.

EXERCISE XVI.

1. I intended to have written it on Saturday.
2. I expected to have heard from him before this.
3. I was in hopes to have finished it before you came.
4. I meant to have told you about it this morning.
5. I found it harder than I thought it would have been.
6. If I had known in time I might have arranged to have gone with you.
7. I don't see that he has done any more than it was his duty to have done.
8. He has formerly been a resident of the town.
9. I am sure that they have been here and did what was required.
10. I have written to him so that he might be ready for us.

11. The fellow scarcely seemed to know that two and two made four.
12. How far did you say it was from Toronto to Montreal?
13. If it was not for that I would go with you.
14. If he received your instructions he would have obeyed them.
15. The chief result of such exertions would have been to have destroyed his health.
16. If he was coming he would be here now.
17. Clerk wanted. It is indispensable that he write a good hand and has some knowledge of book-keeping.
18. If you would take the trouble to look you will see it.
19. If one went unto them from the dead they will repent.
20. I should be obliged to him if he will gratify me in that particular.

VI.—The Coupling of Dissimilar Forms or Constructions.

Reference: Williams, p. 93.

EXERCISE XVII.

1. To do without these things is better than going into debt for them.
2. Ere you mark another's sin,
   Bid thy own conscience look within.
3. I always have and always will uphold that view.
4. Has the committee given in their report yet?
5. The committee who drafted the report were composed of the following members.
6. Here is the book that you lent me, and which I forgot to return yesterday.
7. Persons that read the report, and who do not know him, might think so.
8. I dare say she is as old, if not older than you.
9. He was a better scholar, but not so good a speaker as his friend.

10. This stuff is coarser and in every way inferior to the other.
11. Doth he not leave the ninety and nine and goeth into the wilderness?
12. Did you not promise to help, and even offered to bring your team?
13. Will Mr. H. please excuse John's absence, and oblige, yours truly, A. B.
14. Miss C.'s compliments to Mr. S., and will feel greatly obliged if you will inform me whether, &c.
15. The undersigned has received instructions from the Government Inspector, who has just visited my office, to enforce the regulations.
16. Not having any money, and as I knew no one in the village, I was forced to continue my journey.
17. In this way they learned to steal and many other vices.
18. He promised to find out and that he would send us word.

EXERCISE XVIII.—REVIEW.

1. If I was him I would be ashamed to go there again.
2. The lady tells the little girl that if she should touch that spot with her magic stone she should find great riches.
3. We sorrow not as them that have no hope.
4. Hardly had she entered the car than she discovered her loss.
5. I meant to have given you several of those sort of questions.
6. Hers is one of those impulsive natures that longs for a confidant.
7. There was one man in the town who wanted Silas's money, and that was Dunston Cass, but in order to continue the story, I will have to bring up another family, that of 'Squire Cass.
8. I mean Noah Webster, he that wrote the dictionary.
9. I thought I would have been able to have finished it to-night.
10. The mob appears to have come to their senses at last.

11. He speaks to every one as friendly as if they were his relatives.
12. It will do as good, if not better work, than any machine in the market.
13. A careful examination of all these facts lead to the belief.
14. As I never saw one before I was greatly surprised.
15. One needs to have all their senses about them at such a time.
16. It must have been very difficult to have kept it secret so long.
17. A rhombus is a four-sided figure whose sides are equal, but its angles are not right-angles.
18. Thy thrilling trump had roused the land,
When fraud or danger were at hand.
19. I thought I would have died laughing at his ridiculous appearance.
20. His second proposal was quite different and superior to the first.
21. I could do it easy enough if every one paid their share.
22. I dare say we will find that more than one has had a hand in it.
23. The subscriber has just received a large stock of fresh groceries at his new store on B. St., where I will be happy to wait upon my customers.
24. The prize is to be given to whomsoever will answer the most questions correctly.
25. If he was at home he would give us any quantity of it.
26. These funds will be available for meeting such expenses, and to enable the committee to carry out the scheme properly.
27. It is recommended that he shall be one of the masters of the school, and who shall reside on the premises.
28. It is one of the hardest papers that has ever been given and I will not be surprised if nearly every one of the candidates fail on it.

29. Was it him that argued that the earth was flat?
30. These duties should be performed by an officer whose duties should be defined by the committee, and his salary paid by the Board.
31. We would like to hear how the Company justifies such action, considering their deep indebtedness to us.
32. I was afraid he would have struck me when I told him.
33. They were a very inferior lot compared to the samples.
34. Not a day passes but what more than one is hurt.
35. That would have been a shorter and a simpler method.
36. I have worked it out in full so as all might see the steps.
37. Hardly had the boat started than he saw his mistake.
38. As a consequence both the President and Secretary have resigned.
39. It is one of those phrases that wins immediate assent because it flatters the popular mind.
40. If every one don't do their duty, the battle will certainly be lost.

EXERCISE XIX. — REVIEW.

I. — *Which of the italicized verb-forms in the following sentences would you prefer? Why?*

1. It is I that *is* (*am*) to blame.
2. Three times two *is* (*are*) six.
3. The ebb and flow of the tides *was* (*were*) explained by Newton.
4. More than a century and a half *has* (*have*) elapsed since that.
5. About fifty feet of the bridge *was* (*were*) swept away by the freshet.
6. Ph in such words *has* (*have*) the sound of f.
7. Two and two *makes* (*make*) four.
8. Enough labor and money *has* (*have*) been spent on it already.
9. To invent calumnies and to spread suspicion *requires* (*require*) neither labor nor courage.

10. To admit the existence of such a God and then to refuse to worship him *is* (*are*) surely inconsistent.
11. Riches *does* (*do*) not always bring happiness.
12. Optics *treat* (*treats*) of the laws of light.
13. Great pains *have* (*has*) been taken.
14. The gallows *was* (*were*) erected.
15. The measles *is* (*are*) very prevalent.
16. The public *is* (*are*) cordially invited.
17. The committee *consists* (*consist*) of the following members.
18. There *is* (*are*) not more than another copy of it.
19. Ten dollars *is* (*are*) too much to pay for it.
20. If I *was* (*were*) *he* (*him*) I *would* (*should*) be afraid to try.

II.—*How would you justify the use of the singular verb in the following sentences?*

1. When 9 *is* subtracted from 17 what *is* left?
2. The spectator and historian of the battle *tells* us.
3. Two thousand dollars *was* scarcely sufficient to pay all the expenses.
4. There *was* racing and chasing on Cannobie Lea.
5. A block and tackle *was* made use of in raising it.
6. Wherein *doth* sit the dread and fear of kings.
7. For thine *is* the kingdom and the power and the glory.
8. Happiness, honor, nay life itself, *is* sacrificed in pursuit of it.
9. Early to bed and early to rise
   Makes a man healthy, wealthy, and wise.
10. Every chapter, and indeed every page, *furnishes* proof of this.
11. For a laggard in love and a dastard in war
   Was to wed the fair Ellen of young Lochinvar.
12. It must be one of our opponents that *has* done this.
13. The "Pleasures of Memory" *was* published in 1792.
14. Nine-tenths of it *is* due to drink.
15. That I was present and saw it done *is* quite true.

GOVERNMENT.

I.—Using the Nominative Case after Transitive Verbs and Prepositions.
II.—Using Prepositions after Transitive Verbs.
III.—The Neglect or Misuse of the Possessive Case.

EXERCISE XX.

1. Let you and I go for a pailful of water.
2. I offered to let Mary and she divide it equally.
3. I cannot permit you and he to sit together any longer.
4. You may appoint whoever you like.
5. Who were you talking to just now?
6. Who did you expect to see?
7. Can't you remember who you gave it to?
8. Between you and I it looks rather suspicious.
9. He left word for John and I to call on our way home.
10. Girls like you and she ought to be ashamed to act so.
11. I mentioned it to those whom I met, and she among the rest.
12. There seems to be nobody here but you and I.
13. All the girls had gone except her and I.
14. He refused to accept of any remuneration for his services.
15. I will not allow of such conduct in this room.
16. I don't recollect of any similar instance.
17. I remember of hearing him make the statement.
18. He will not permit of any interruption.
19. Who was that lady standing near you and I?
20. There is no use in me trying the examination.
21. Is there any prospect of the Council passing such a by-law?
22. A dog and a cat's head are differently shaped.
23. Whose dictionary do you prefer? Webster, or Worcester?
24. It is neither the steward nor the purser's duty.

EXERCISE XXI.—REVIEW.

1. I did not succeed quite so well as I wished to have done.
2. I don't know as the exact cost is known yet.
3. You are not the first boy that have made that mistake.
4. But the worst of it is that he don't seem to care at all whether he does real good or not.
5. At the head of the party was Fox and Lord Grey.
6. Each of the candidates pledged themselves to abide by his decision.
7. That remark must have been intended for you and I.
8. It is one of the worst cases that has come under my notice.
9. If I was her I would be afraid of him finding out who done it.
10. He professed to believe that the soul perished with the body.
11. He refused to comply to the demand of the Board.
12. Neither by you or he was it seemingly regarded as necessary.
13. The committee which was appointed to consider the matter have brought in a long report.
14. I don't see but what you have as good a right to it as her.
15. I would have liked very much to have had a talk with him.
16. When a person makes such a mistake they generally try to conceal it.
17. The "Elegy" is one of the few poems that is not injured by constant repetition.
18. He knows as much, if not more, Greek than most graduates.
19. Neither of us had any mistakes in our exercises.
20. I would probably have gone independent of his offer.
21. But how different was it at Rareloe than it might have been.
22. I don't care who I work for as long as I get my pay.
23. I soon found out that I was at first on the wrong track and began to get better acquainted with History, studying it some harder.
24. It, as well as several of the others, seem to have been carelessly done.

25. I cannot excuse those whose business it was to have attended to it.
26. It makes no difference whom you thought it was.
27. What will be the consequence if the examination papers were made easier or more mechanical?
28. The amount of all these alterations and additions are so great as to make it look like a new book.
29. Telegraph me directly you reach Buffalo.
30. I thought I spoke plain enough on that point yesterday.
31. Each of you are entitled to the third of the money.
32. I wish it wasn't so far from here to the office.
33. He agreed to vote for whoever the convention would nominate.
34. Every citizen, old or young, should demand their rights.
35. He is probably the best known of any other American politician in England.
36. The Journal has the largest circulation of any other paper in the state.
37. The winter has not been as severe as we expected it would have been.
38. His prices are less than any grocer in town.
39. Not one of these men offered to lend their assistance.
40. He wouldn't go without we did.
41. The eldest of the two girls attends the High School.
42. He remembered the names of most of the authors and books of which we had been speaking.
43. No one could have acted fairer than her.
44. Scarcely one in twenty could write their names.
45. He was seated at the table with a glass of ale on both sides of him.
46. Both the beginning and end of the book were torn out.
47. I wouldn't have acted like you did for twice the money.
48. One after another withdrew their opposition.
49. I fear we will all feel the need for warmer clothing.
50. Any one that likes can leave their books here till they are going home.

POSITION.

The Misplacement of Conjunctions, Adverbs, Adverbial Phrases, and Relative Clauses.

References: Longmans, the chapter On the Arrangement of Words, beginning with section 139, especially 187 ff. and 193–196; Williams, pp. 81, 82. The general principle, which the student should be sure to master, is this: "Words closely related in thought should be placed together, words distinct in thought kept apart." See Wendell's *English Composition*, pp. 104 ff.

EXERCISE XXII.

1. He both taught them to read and to write.
2. He neither answered my letter nor my card.
3. He was not competent either to teach classics or mathematics.
4. Such a task would be alike barren of instruction and amusement.
5. It will not merely interest the children, but also the parents.
6. You are not only mistaken in your inferences, but also in your facts.
7. I have only received one letter from her since she left.
8. He only rents the store, not the house.
9. His dexterity almost appeared miraculous.
10. He must have wanted to see them very much.
11. I forgot to sign my name to a letter once.
12. I fear that it will be necessary to entirely remodel it.[1]
13. I beg to respectfully recommend its adoption.
14. I scarcely ever remember hearing one that I liked better.
15. Everybody thought that it was destined to be a great city, twenty years ago.
16. He rose speedily in his employer's estimation, who very much respected him.

---

[1] See Earle's *English Prose* (New York: Putnam's Sons, 1891), pp. 182–186, for a statement of the rapid progress towards good use of this innovation, to which Mr. Earle assigns as cause "an instinctive effort to satisfy the desire for lucidity."

17. He is unworthy of the confidence of a fellow-being that disregards the laws of his Maker.
18. Bosworth was the last battle of the wars of the Roses in which Richard the Third was slain.
19. I fear you will find it rather an unpleasant task.[1]
20. I can neither find him nor his brother.
21. The judge sentenced him to jail for disorderly conduct for ten days.

EXERCISE XXIII. — REVIEW.

1. He invented some sort of a machine for the purpose.
2. The schools are very different now to what they were then.
3. That was the mayor, as well as the sheriff's opinion.
4. Neither of the books that you seen laying on the floor were mine.
5. It was his duty to have corrected the error at once.
6. At least ten thousand dollars worth of property were destroyed by the fire.
7. It is as cold, if not colder, than any day last winter.
8. It may have been Mr. A. and not her that done it.
9. The Board has appointed Mr. M. to audit their accounts.
10. Who do you think Mary and her met on their way home?
11. If I was to remove this weight what would happen?
12. I have been told that he don't visit them often.
13. He acknowledged that he intended to have used it.
14. Shakespeare is more true to nature than any writer I know of.
15. Every day, and in fact every hour, bring their changes.
16. No people was ever more fiercely assailed by persecution than those of this country.
17. The junior classes are, if not better, at least as well taught as the senior ones.
18. The family with whom she has been boarding has decided to return to Michigan.[2]

---

[1] Consult a dictionary on this point.

[2] See above, p. 6, note 2.

19. Will either of you girls lend this boy your slate?
20. His long experience, joined to his natural aptitude for teaching, enable him to accomplish this.
21. Nobody but you and I know where to find them.
22. You must learn to carefully distinguish between these two forms.
23. He was not only noted for his theoretical knowledge, but also for his practical skill.
24. Neither he or his wife seem to care what sort of an example they set their children.
25. The meaning of words, phrases, and sentences are taken up with the class before reading the lesson.
26. I have very little hope of him passing the examination.
27. You should not accept of such an excuse.
28. At that time Mexico was both more populous and more civilized than any country in America.
29. The same wind detained the king's fleet in their station at Harwich.
30. It affords the opportunity of considering whether his purpose in establishing the school, and which has so far remained unfulfilled, cannot now be carried out.
31. What kind of an adjective did you say *all* was?
32. But for you and I he would have had to have gone alone.
33. I don't think he acted quite fair to his brother-in-laws.
34. He only offered me thirty dollars for it.
35. M. & Co. claim to sell cheaper than any store in town.
36. Where will I find such another friend?
37. If it was there I would certainly have seen it.
38. It is used both as a transitive and intransitive verb.
39. He answered all the questions that were put to him quite readily.
40. Mr. M., of whom you must have heard and may perhaps have seen, is said to be the author.
41. Each of these pieces were then cut into three others.
42. Most of them were as large if not larger than this.

43. It only made them fight fiercer than ever.
44. He must have went in the house before you came.
45. It is one of the best books that has been written on the subject.
46. For the next week nothing but balls and parties were talked of.
47. They were all curious to know whom the writer could have been.
48. I will be able to show you that there is many other points of resemblance between them. .
49. They found that the river had raised in the night and overflown the lot.
50. You can keep this letter and show it to whoever you like.

MISCELLANEOUS SYNTACTICAL ERRORS.

I. — Double Negatives. II. — Ellipsis. III. — Pleonasm.

References: Williams, pp. 56 (section 3), 106; Longmans, sections 85, 86, 307, 374.

EXERCISE XXIV.

1. Neither you nor nobody else ever saw me do it.
2. Henceforth I cannot nor will not make any allowance in such cases.
3. The council has not now, nor never had the power to pass such a by-law.
4. He didn't leave any here, I don't think.
5. He isn't likely to come by this train, I don't suppose.
6. There wasn't hardly anybody there that I knew.
7. No two teachers could hardly differ more in style.
8. The past and present condition of Greece are very different.
9. The determining the boundary line is the most important matter.
10. For sale, a Dictionary and Atlas, both nearly new.
11. There isn't one that can't read, and few that can't write.

12. The man who was left in charge of it and attends to it is beginning to wonder what has happened.
13. He has got a good deal more to do this term.[1]
14. He will be here in the latter end of next week.
15. He was a child of ten years old at the time.
16. His two sisters were both at the meeting.
17. The funeral will take place at three p.m. to-morrow afternoon.
18. She met in with them on her way home.
19. There are generally a good many go to them.
20. His mother was a poor widow woman.[2]
21. Lend me the loan of your ruler for a little while.
22. I know not from whence he came, or where he went to.
23. Whenever I see her she always asks about you.
24. Before you go you must first finish your exercise.
25. I came as fast as ever I could.
26. It is a good plan to adopt with new beginners.
27. He did it equally as well as his friends.
28. It must be ten years ago since he left home.
29. I haven't gone and I'm not going to.
30. No one has ever been able to explain it, and probably never will.

COMMON IMPROPRIETIES AND VULGARISMS.

EXERCISE XXV.

1. She looked kind of surprised when she found you here.[3]
2. I sort of thought you would come to-night.
3. I am just after writing to him for some more.
4. He hadn't ought to have told her about it.
5. She would not stay, being as how she was all alone.
6. He told me that he used to could do that.

---

[1] On *got* consult *The Century Dictionary*.

[2] Compare 2 Sam. xiv. 5, and *King John* ii. 1. 548.

[3] See above, p. 4, note 2.

7. He would have gone home if I had not have stopped him.
8. I see them most every day.
9. He was some better when we left him this morning.
10. He came very near being drowned.
11. The dog attackted him on the street.
12. He left home unbeknown to his parents.
13. The doctor wasn't to home when I called.
14. This here answer aint correct.
15. That there boy don't seem to be attending.
16. Tell that hind boy to sit down.
17. Whatever did you do that for?
18. She lives quite a long ways from the school.

EXERCISE XXVI. — REVIEW.

1. Was it a man or a woman's voice that we heard?
2. In what State did you say Chicago was?
3. Such a course is likely to be attended by much danger.
4. No one in England knew what tea was five hundred years ago.
5. These girls will neither listen nor let nobody else listen.
6. Neither you or I are in the wrong.
7. You will not find him to home this morning, I don't think.
8. There is need of institutions like U. C. College ought to be.
9. I left this school on account of my family moving to the country.
10. Any boy with any sense in their head would have known the difference.
11. Men are in the plural number because they mean several.
12. Wanted, a nurse and housemaid, who must both have good references.
13. His method of solving it was quite different to mine.
14. It seems to me that you have weakened instead of strengthening your case.
15. He is only fitted to govern others who can govern himself.
16. Neither Paine nor Voltaire were able to advance any new objections.

17. The party who are to be invited is both numerous and select.
18. He never has and probably never will forgive me for deceiving him.
19. Its last statements are quite as reckless, and even more malicious than its former ones.
20. He was not only accused of theft, but also of murder.
21. All males are of the masculine gender, and females of the feminine.
22. If he don't come be sure and let me know.
23. I would have been there by this time if you hadn't have delayed me.
24. Nothing but balls and parties seem to have any interest for her.
25. You can go as soon as you are done your exercise.
26. There is over one hundred buildings gone up since last spring.
27. What is to prevent him finding out who done it?
28. Hoping that I will hear from you soon believe me yours, etc.
29. I felt kind of frightened at first.
30. He said it was her that begun it.
31. When a nation forms a government it is power, not wisdom, which they place in the hands of that government.
32. You wasn't paying attention to the explanation, I don't think.
33. The committee is to meet at 10 A.M. on Wednesday forenoon.
34. Nobody but the doctor and the nurse are allowed to see him.
35. Wont he be surprised to find that we aint going?
36. Each of you boys have got as much as you can carry.
37. Has the jury brought in their verdict yet?
38. Try and remember where you left it laying.
39. Many of our best scholars lack that knowledge of business affairs which are so essential to success.
40. This part of his description had better have been omitted.[1]

[1] The expression *had better* is not incorrect, but it should be carefully looked up. See *The Century Dictionary* under *have*, i. 14; the *New English Diction-*

41. He said he didn't know as that would affect it.
42. I scarcely ever remember seeing a finer sunset.
43. That's the boy whom most of them thought would get it.
44. I thought of returning several times, but felt ashamed to give up.
45. Mr. G. is continuing the war against the company by means of injunctions and mandami.
46. I shall not punish you for breaking it, but for lying.
47. No motion shall be received, except to adjourn, or to lie on the table.
48. Let us hope that the boys will come home with a good account of the kite's conduct to their father.
49. There are others whose names we could give that have shook the clay of Dakota from their feet, and bade adieu to that country.
50. Thinks I to myself, "This is a queer sort of a place."[1]
51. It's part of your duty to learn them how to do it.
52. He said for us to leave it at the house if he wasn't to home.
53. He had ought to be ashamed of what he done yesterday.
54. In this way books are folded and stitched without being handled scarcely.
55. The pupil must be carefully trained to note the difference between the adjective and adverb.
56. I have no doubt but what he felt kind of disappointed.
57. We have come to the conclusion that we will not accept his offer.
58. The mud on the streets was perfectly awful.
59. I expect that he had forgotten to tell her.
60. I would not have thought it would take that long.
61. When he went back for to pick it up it was gone.
62. I am afraid that the poor boy don't know no better.
63. There is both a large and small dictionary in the library.

---

ary under *better*, i. 4. *b*. It is thoroughly discussed by Fitzedward Hall in *Modern English*.

[1] Decide for yourself whether "thinks I to myself" is or is not idiomatic English.

64. I am sure we will all be very pleased to hear of it.
65. Not only Mr. A., but even your brother were induced to believe it.
66. He aint likely to give us another chance, I don't suppose.
67. Haven't you no idea who done it?
68. He wasn't a boy whom any of us thought would do such a thing.
69. He offered me the lend of a bag to put them in.
70. He is stopping with us and he finds it sort of lonesome.
71. One of the girls that goes to the Model school gave it to me.
72. Who were you talking to when Mary and me passed you?
73. The youngest of the two is not more than ten, I don't think.
74. Most every one in the room thought it was plenty long enough.
75. He lives as far, if not farther from the church than you do.
76. He jumped onto the sleigh and drove off at full speed.
77. You can take any sheets that aint marked.
78. Neither he nor no one else have any right to touch it.
79. I wish you to understand that I am not doing this for fun, but for profit.
80. Trusting to hear from you soon, believe me yours truly.
81. I never want to be in the same fix again.[1]
82. The truth is, she don't go to school very regular.
83. It aint very likely that you will find them to home.
84. I only want the lend of it for a few minutes.
85. The poet was not only deprived of his land, but barely escaped with his life.
86. Shakespeare's name is spelled in I don't know how many ways, and Raleigh's in no less.
87. Pupils should not be asked to write on such subjects without they have access to a library.
88. If I had only have thought of it sooner I would have been able to have gone too.
89. All I've got to say is that I will be very surprised if he don't pass.

---

[1] Consult the dictionaries on this point.

90. That question has not and probably never will be satisfactorily settled.
91. The undersigned has now in stock fifty sets, all of our own manufacture.
92. Neither the chairman nor the secretary would give their consent.
93. It is to this feature of the bill to which I wish to draw your attention.
94. With this machine you can make two hundred copies of anything that can be written on a page of note paper in five minutes.
95. I never have nor never will agree to such a proposal.
96. The "Elegy" is one of the few poems that is not injured by constant repetition.
97. The Board has been fortunate enough to secure the services of a gentleman who will see that their instructions are carried out.
98. He should be exercised in quoting passages of special beauty from the selections prescribed, and to reproduce the substance of them in his own words.
99. Candidates must be careful only to use such contractions as are generally used, or which cannot be mistaken.

EXERCISE XXVII. — REVIEW.

1. —*Justify or correct (giving reasons) the form of the italicized words in the following sentences:* —

1. I am a plain, blunt man that *love my* friend.
2. It is you and not your brother that *deserves* to be blamed.
3. And many a holy text around she strews,
   That *teach* the rustic moralist to die.
4. My robe and my integrity to heaven *is* all I dare now call my own.
5. Nine-tenths of all that misery *is* caused by idleness.

6. A generous troop *appears*
Who *spread their* bucklers and *advance their* spears.
7. There *is* a tribe in these mountains who *are* fairer colored and more intelligent than the rest of the natives.
8. Mathematics *is* regarded as of more importance than English.
9. His marks in the different subjects were as *follows*.
10. I have ventured *this* many summers in a sea of glory.[1]
11. There is no doubt of its being *she*.
12. He brought home three *pair* of shoes.
13. I bought it from Mr. A., than *whom* there isn't a better judge in the city.[2]
14. Nodding *their* heads before her *goes* the merry minstrelsy.
15. *Who* do you suppose he took me to be?
16. *Who* does he think it could have been?
17. Do I understand your Worship to say that *you* think, etc.?

II.—*Distinguish in meaning between,*—

1. Much depends on the teacher (teacher's) correcting the papers.
2. Just think of him (his) engaging in such work.
3. He was an abler statesman than (a) soldier.
4. She sings as well as (she) plays.
5. One of the causes that has (have) not been mentioned is the following.
6. He took great pains to explain (in explaining) everything.
7. He was careful to work out (in working out) the question for them.
8. He expressed the pleasure he felt in hearing a story of him (of his).

---

[1] *Henry VIII.*, iii. 2, 360. See Schmidt, *Shakespeare-Lexicon*, under *this*.

[2] "A noun or pronoun after *than* has a show of analogy with one governed by a preposition, and is sometimes blunderingly put in the objective case even when of subjective value; as, none knew better than him. Even Milton says *than whom*, and this is more usual; for example, *than whom* there is none better."—*The Century Dictionary*, under *than*.

9. If I have (had) (had had) the book I, etc.
10. If he did it he would (should) be punished.
11. If he was (were) present what should I do?
12. I remember an anecdote of the doctor (doctor's) which may interest you.
13. William and John's books. William's and John's books.
14. He merely glanced at the answer. He glanced at the answer merely.
15. He stood still, watching them. He stood, still watching them. He still stood, watching them.
16. Mr. S., also, expressed the opinion that, etc. Mr. S. also expressed the opinion that, etc. Mr. S. expressed the opinion also, that, etc.
17. If he goes I go. If he go I shall go.
18. If he has (have) it he will give it to you.
19. He lived (has lived) there for forty years.
20. Who gave it to you? Which gave it to you?
21. I will go if he asks me. I would go if he asked me.
22. Are you going (coming) to the meeting?
23. Are (aren't) you going to it?
24. Even Tom offered to help. Tom even offered to help.

MISCELLANEOUS GRAMMATICAL ERRORS.

EXERCISE XXVIII.—REVIEW.

1. It wasn't her that done it, I don't think.
2. Which is the cheapest, to go by Toronto, or by Hamilton?
3. There is no two of them exactly alike.
4. But for you and I he would have been drownded.
5. He would have laid there all night, if we had not have wakened him.
6. Can I leave my seat for a few minutes?
7. Is there any one in the class that don't understand it?

8. Who did you give the parcel to?
9. Her and I can carry it easy enough.
10. If any pupil has seen anything of it I will be glad if they will let me know.
11. Each candidate must provide their own stationery.
12. How will I know who to give it to?
13. We don't want no loafers here.
14. There is surely some other places of importance.
15. Wasn't you awfully glad to get home?
16. Whom did he say had been appointed secretary?
17. Bosworth was the last battle of the wars of the Roses, in which Richard III. was slain.
18. He don't seem to bowl as good as he used to.
19. He is just as honest, if not more so, than any of his neighbors.
20. Two teaspoonsful of the mixture, dissolved in a glass of water and drank during effervescence, makes a cooling drink.
21. I have not heard of anybody but the Smith's that are invited.
22. It was so dark that I couldn't see the horses, hardly.
23. They seem to me to be nearly dressed alike.
24. What did he say the name of this station was?
25. There is no chance of him passing without he works harder.
26. It ain't likely that I will be able to finish it to-day.
27. Who do you think we met this morning?
28. What have you got in your hand?
29. I meant to have written it this morning.
30. Have either of you a copy of the questions that was given at the last examination?
31. I would have done it as cheap as him if you had asked me.
32. You will seldom or ever find him to home in the evening.
33. Probably more than one teacher present has met with such cases.
34. That place ain't marked on the map, I don't think.
35. I think it must be some sort of a fever.
36. Nobody but you and she were in the room since.
37. I don't see that he either has or can gain anything by it.

38. Where would we find any one willing to go to so much trouble?
39. He asked me if he could not have the use of it for a few days.
40. I intended to have insisted on this sympathy at greater length.
41. It is one of the most interesting articles that has appeared in the "Monthly."
42. I sold them to Johnson, he that has a shop on W. St.
43. Neither Holmes nor Thompson were class-mates of mine.
44. Let every one attend to their own slates.
45. He thinks that what he don't know ain't worth knowing.
46. I have heard nothing of it, neither from him or his friends.
47. I prefer to wait for him than to go alone.
48. You can't deny but what you received notice.
49. He seemed to have every confidence of his ability to finish it.
50. That needn't make any difference between old friends like you and I.
51. If you had been working all the morning like we have you would be glad to rest.
52. Nobody but you and I seem to know about it.
53. Sixteen multiplied by six equals to what?
54. As surely as we pass them by, as surely as we leave them to themselves, will we pay, will our descendants pay, for our selfish heedlessness.
55. I had a better opinion of you than to have supposed that you would do such a thing.
56. Little more but the names of the authors and their works are given in the notes.
57. It isn't one of the words that adds *es* in the plural.
58. Neither the Old or New Testament contain any such verse.
59. I will have to go alone without he changes his mind.
60. Are you not near done your exercise yet?
61. I don't hardly think he will come to-night.
62. Would there be any use in us going to see him about it?
63. Her and I agreed to write to one another every week.
64. A large quantity of military stores and provisions were found in the fort.

65. Who was Cortez sent out by?
66. If any person is not satisfied with the pictures I will refund them their money.
67. I'm just after explaining to the class how to work those sort of questions.
68. Wasn't you at school the day it was broke?
69. We can't wait no longer for them boys.
70. Boys like you and he ought to be ashamed to behave so bad in church.
71. It has been a matter of astonishment for me to get from you as pure and excellent a brand of Tokay as can only be got at the court of Vienna.
72. This letter is from my cousin Annie, she that you met here last summer.
73. See that none are admitted whom you think will not be true to the cause.
74. It is very likely that there was more than one concerned in it.
75. Such prices are only paid in times of great scarcity.
76. He spoke so slow and distinct that I caught every word.
77. Neither Selden nor Bacon were graduates of a University.
78. I kind of thought he might have taken it.
79. If you had went home and asked her perhaps she would have let you come with Jane and I.
80. They were certainly very far removed from having been guilty of a conscious deception.
81. Every intelligent mechanic ought to use their influence on his behalf.
82. You never have, and I trust you never will, meet with such a trial.
83. There is no doubt but what he expected to have been first.
84. I told him he could stop at home this afternoon if he liked.
85. But, after all, these are nothing when compared to the advantages it offers.
86. She couldn't answer a single question, scarcely.
87. I won't allow of any interference with my authority.

88. If I was in his place I would be glad to get rid of it.
89. I will try and do it.
90. I look on it as one of the most feasible schemes that has been proposed.
91. She had forgot to tell him that the flour was nearly gone.
92. There ain't a book in the library, hardly, but what he has read.
93. Who does he think the association is likely to appoint as their agent here?
94. I was in hopes to have seen you at the party last night.
95. In short, I have heard of nobody except an actor and a doctor of divinity that profess their esteem for my odes.
96. Is their any one in the class that don't understand how to fill up their form?
97. Be sure and let me know if the water raises any higher.
98. My prices will be found as low, if not lower, than can be found elsewhere.
99. My stock is more complete than ever, and our customers may rest assured at getting bargains.
100. In her name has been committed some of the vilest crimes which stain the page of history.
101. You can take any that you can find laying on the counter.
102. The spirit, and not the letter, of the law, are what we ought to look at.
103. It don't seem possible that you have such another chance.
104. His idea was that one which in some respects had been desired by Danton and Lamartine.
105. Mr. H. is one of those who won scholarships but was refused payment.
106. More than one outbreak with typhoid fever has been due to such a state of affairs.
107. It wasn't me that done it; it was that there boy.
108. This cake tastes quite nicely, after all, don't it?
109. I can't understand how any one can keep their temper.
110. I worked steady at my trade for full two years.

111. He told us there was two principal propositions in the sentence.
112. He said he would give it to whomsoever would solve the equation first.
113. Suppose that he was to come in and find you acting so disorderly.
114. He had no other course open to him but to resign, and which he accordingly did.
115. He hasn't gone and ain't likely to.
116. They will be interested when the nature of a syllogism or the fallacy of a proposition are explained to them.
117. In such matters profusion as well as parsimony are to be avoided.
118. The rising and falling inflection require to be carefully distinguished.
119. No one would write a book unless he thinks it will be read.
120. She surely don't expect me to tell who I got it from.
121. His machine works quite different to what I expected.
122. Are either of these places marked on the map?
123. He may even succeed to make out the sense of the passage.
124. She then bid good-by to Basil, who returned to his home.
125. It is said to be homogeneous when the sum of the indices are the same.
126. The inscription gave the name and age of the deceased merely.
127. I have lost the game, though it seemed to me as if I should have won it.
128. One night he was befallen by a greater misfortune than ever before.
129. You have got no right to open it without permission.
130. Mrs. A.'s compliments to Mr. B., and would you be kind enough to send me a list of the books required.
131. When one tries their hand at predicting, it is best not to be too definite.

132. Wanted, a short-hand writer, by a legal firm, who can also engross well.
133. It is one of the greatest misfortunes that has or can happen to the town.
134. In spite of all his efforts he could not assimilate himself to book-keeping.
135. Is it ignorance or carelessness that are the cause of him failing so often?
136. Was it her that was talking so loud in the next room?
137. You will never succeed to pass the examination without you are more careful.
138. He told me that you had gone to the city, and wasn't to be back till Wednesday.
139. He has no farther need for it, and neither have I.
140. What avails all these advantages if he will not profit from them?
141. Each of us could furnish instances from our own experience.
142. I know of no one better fitted for it, or so likely to give satisfaction, as Mr. M.
143. The committee trusts that the citizens will co-operate heartily with them in making the entertainment a success.
144. He hasn't a bit of strength, no more than an infant.
145. He seemed to thoroughly understand the subject.
146. This celebrated and popular medicine will cure catarrh quicker than any remedy offered to the public.
147. If it wasn't for the newspapers we would know very little of what is going on around us.
148. Neither my brother nor I were able to endure it any longer.
149. The arranging the programme will take some time.
150. Had I known sooner I would have been able to have made arrangements for him to have stopped with us.
151. A few inches more or less in a lady's height makes a great difference.
152. You must speak plainer if you wish to be understood.

153. Unless a teacher feels that he or she has a divine mission in the work, they are not likely to succeed.
154. There is a great difference between the present and past condition of the school.
155. Winter in our temperate climate exhibits very few phenomena in comparison to what is visible in the Arctic regions.
156. He said that he should like that the matter would be definitely settled.
157. If not larger, it certainly is quite as large as the specimen which you showed us yesterday.
158. No two positions in life could hardly be more opposite.
159. I don't suppose there was any one in the room but what suspected something.
160. Every tree and every shrub glittered in the sunlight as if they were covered with diamonds.
161. As I never saw a play before, it proved very interesting.
162. Unfortunately he neither knows the name or the residence of the owner.
163. A gentleman living on West Street, and who is a frequent visitor in our office, handed it to us.
164. 'Tis thine to command, mine to obey; let me know therefore what your orders are.
165. It had been his intention, I believe, to have received us with considerable ceremony.
166. Any who has seen it will admit that we have not, and, indeed, can not, do it justice.
167. I see why you do that quite clearly, but I don't understand the next step.
168. I indeed prefer a man without money than money without a man.
169. The derivation of the word, as well as the usage of our best writers, are in favor of this view.
170. There have been three famous talkers in England, either of whom would serve as an illustration.

171. He has come a long ways expressly for to try the examination.
172. If he was to find out that it was her who wrote it he would be very angry.
173. Yet no sooner does morning dawn but the strange enchantment vanishes.
174. You was taken up too much with the thoughts to notice the language with which they were clothed.
175. Every one of the witnesses gave it as their opinion that neither the captain or the mate were to blame for the accident.
176. There is also a council who, though itself irresponsible, governs the educational interests of the Province.
177. He was a man who, though I did not like him, I could not help respecting.
178. We will find that all the most common and useful words, as well as the greater part of the grammar, is native.
179. You can scarcely find a more universal blunder.
180. There are occasions in the life of nearly every one when they cannot find words to adequately express their feelings.
181. A proper diphthong is when both vowels are sounded.
182. It contains a great deal that is useful, and which may be turned to good account.
183. The committee pays the town authorities a high tribute for the courtesy and attention which was shown them during their visit.
184. I ain't sure which of the two is the largest.
185. More than one of the candidates seemed anxious to show off his knowledge.
186. To test that I would need to have given the class a written examination.
187. A hasty perusal of this strange production might not show you that it was a poem.
188. The greatest number of candidates came up to that examination of any former year.

189. The crown of England can only be worn by a Protestant.
190. If it wasn't for you and she, and two or three more, I would leave.
191. Emphasis is the laying a greater stress on some words than on others.
192. He struck me as I was jumping onto the sleigh.
193. The court has taken a different view than did the public, and have awarded him a considerable sum.
194. He has just issued his thousandth and first volume.
195. I have very little doubt but what you might find some of them laying around yet, if you would take the trouble to look for them.
196. He looks on it as one of the most admirable military performances that has taken place in modern times.
197. The manufacture of them has now arrived to immense proportions.
198. Neither the power to issue a license, nor the power to regulate, were questions before the court.
199. No professional man, no business man,—in fact, no man of sense,—would risk their reputation by supporting such a scheme.
200. We are convinced that were the question brought before the Privy Council it will be found that these powers belong to the Local Legislatures.
201. If I succeed to discharge the duties devolving on me, satisfactorily, it will be because, etc.
202. There are generally a good many go from mere curiosity.
203. He is one of the few who can be depended on to keep his presence of mind on such occasions.
204. Egypt would scarcely have been able to have secured her independence by her own efforts.
205. Color-blindness is so common in some countries that nearly one in every twenty of the inhabitants suffer from it.
206. I know of no method that will accomplish this so effectually, or at less expense, than that you have suggested.

207. Like Shakespeare his genius is sublime, and his imagination unbounded.
208. Though her disposition was quite different and superior to his, many causes contributed to render her less popular than him.
209. A. and B. beg to announce that they have commenced business in the above store. Having purchased our stock at close prices, we are prepared to offer bargains.
210. After the jury was in the box he wanted to challenge several of them whom he said had a prejudice against his client.
211. The captain admitted that he had several of his crew died with yellow fever.
212. It is one of the greatest mistakes that has been made by England in dealing with the natives.
213. At the expiration of the time every one must read what they have written.
214. Short as this gospel is, it tells us many things not contained in either of the other three.
215. Not returning at the usual hour, the family became alarmed, and a party was organized to search for them.
216. The future of England depends on each generation showing the same courage, wisdom, and moderation as was shown by those who made her what she is.
217. Resolved: That this society desires to record its conviction that by the removal of C. D. we have lost one of our most active and useful members.
218. Michigan and New Hampshire are the only States electing gubernatorial candidates who have declared for the Republicans.
219. The new hotel belonging to Mr. C., and which was only recently opened to the public, was burned last night.
220. The indebtedness of the English language to the Greek, Latin, and French, is disclosed on every page.
221. One night last week the house of D. W. of this town was

entered by a burglar, which for cool audacity is seldom beaten.

222. The gentleman must remember that the road was not built simply that he may enjoy a large salary as Managing Director.

223. The Prime Minister with the Chancellor of the Exchequer were admitted to her presence.

224. It is stronger and every way superior to the other one.

225. He said it was a great misfortune that men of letters seldom looked on the practical side of such matters.

226. Personification is when we ascribe life or action to inanimate objects.

227. Nearly every one of the teachers present gave it as their opinion that there was more than one way of interpreting the question, and that consequently neither of the three answers were absolutely wrong.

228. It is much to be regretted that they should, as they have, elected him for their representative.

229. Mrs. A.'s compliments to Mrs. B., and begs to state that Mary C. lived with me nearly a year, and that I found her capable and honest.

230. He said that he had heard nothing, and did not expect to, before Saturday.

231. His reputation is equal to any writer in the country.

232. He appeared to clearly understand the various steps of the process.

233. I am one of those people who cannot describe what I have not seen.

234. Did you not agree to sell it to me for $20, and offered to wait three months for your pay?

235. If we were to examine them under a microscope we would find that not one of all these crystals were alike.

236. It is no use in us reasoning any longer with him.

237. In place of the old list I have prepared another, and which I think will be found more useful.

238. He had made so many alterations and additions to the plan that I scarcely recognized it.

239. I am not going to speak in favor of my second thoughts in comparison of my first, but against scepticism, etc.

240. At this time the Board of Agriculture was employed in completing their valuable series of county reports.

241. A rapid increase in the number of schools and of the pupils attending them are not at present to be expected.

242. Parties wishing a selection should telegraph, as the goods will not remain long in stock, in order to prevent disappointment.

243. The House of Commons, which represented the middle classes, were apparently afraid, etc.

244. It is surely preferable to die the death of a patriot than to live the life of a slave.

245. If thou bring thy gift to the altar, and there rememberest, etc. (Matt. v. 24.)

246. Irving and Macaulay's style are very different.

247. Presently I came to a bog into which I knew if I strayed I would never emerge unaided.

248. Now is the time to raise our school into such a state of efficiency that will enable it to prepare pupils for the various Universities.

249. These passages will confirm what I say, and which has only to be stated to be acknowledged by any Bible student.

250. No subject has engaged the time and attention of teachers so much, or been more pressed upon them by parents, than reading.

251. This hypothesis, as well as those previously referred to, merely prove the hallucination of the authors.

252. It may be employed to strengthen the impression which we intend that any object should make.

253. If he was wise he would have contented himself to follow their advice.

254. It appears that no one is exempt from serving on a coroner's jury, and may be fined for non-attendance.

255. To-morrow being the last day of the Regatta, and on which takes place the races of the Rowing Club, will doubtless attract a large crowd.

256. The last hitch in this celebrated case appears to be the most absurd of all its predecessors.

257. None of the readers appeared, and what is more indefensible, failed to procure substitutes.

258. As much, and, indeed, sometimes greater evil, is caused by neglect of duty than by mal-performance of it.

259. The party, though disgraced by the corruption of its leaders, made a strong effort to regain their former ascendency.

260. He is a person whom we all feel sure will represent the college both with honor to himself and to all concerned.

261. Christian and Moor in death promiscuous lay,
Each where they fell.

262. No principles can be stated, nor no rules laid down, that will apply to all these sort of questions.

263. The two things to be kept in view are the proper training of the children while they are in the Home, and the finding employment for them when they leave it.

264. If he were guilty of such conduct, and there seems to be no doubt of it, he deserves all the censure that has been passed upon him.

265. Just to thy word, in every thought sincere,
Who knew no wish but what the world might hear.

266. There will be no obstacle to his retaining command of a regiment with which his name has long been identified, and to whose untiring zeal and attention it owes much of its present efficiency.

267. Who art thou? Speak! that on designs unknown,
While others sleep, thus range the camps alone.

268. Did ever Proteus, Merlin, or any witch
Transform themselves so strangely as the rich.

269. If English orthography represented English pronunciation as closely as the Italian does, at least half the time and expense of teaching to read and spell would be saved.

270. O fairest flower! no sooner blown but blasted!

271. Thou who didst call the Furies from th' abyss,
And round Orestes bade them howl and hiss.

272. It is not one of those physical theories which, as Tyndall says, lies beyond experience, but is yet derived by a process of abstraction from experience.

273. No sensible man believes, and has not since the *News* left the *Mail* building, that there is any connection between the two papers.

274. What shall we say, since silent now is he,
Who, when he spake, all things would silent be?

275. No undergraduate can obtain these distinctions without passing examinations of such a character as to prove that mere mechanical knowledge will not suffice to secure them the literary warrant of a degree.

276. Nor one of all the race was known,
But prized its weal above their own.

277. I might further show design in the formation of flowers, as well as in the behavior of plants after fertilization had been effected and the seeds ripening.

278. If there is anything that was abhorrent to me, it was the scattering doubts and unsettling consciences without necessity.

279. The biographer testifies that while Baxter lived in an age of voluminous authorship, he was, beyond all comparison, the most voluminous of all his contemporaries.

280. The sale of these patterns in Canada have been more than all others combined, and if the increase continues I will again have to double my facilities.

281. Like the leaves of the forest, when summer is green,
That host, with their banners, at sunset was seen.

282. Each looked to the sun, and stream, and plain,
As what they ne'er might see again.

283. Praise from a friend, or censure from a foe,
Are lost on hearers who our merits know.

284. It seems that he had never before had the good fortune to have seen one.

285. His administration was undoubtedly the least oppressive of that of any of the French Generals in the Peninsula.

286. It may put him in the way of commencing aright, and inspiring him to continue his researches into the principles of Education.

287. Students who have partially completed their studies elsewhere, and having satisfactory evidence of the fact, will be placed in advanced classes.

288. I expect that in a short time I will be in a position to fully acquaint the public of the reasons of this action on his part.

289. C. and E. return thanks to their friends and the public generally for their liberal support in the past, and we wish one and all a happy and prosperous New Year.

290. In short, he has received such instruction, and had such practice as enables him to begin aright for himself when he goes into a school, and further serves as a guide to direct his future studies.

291. A sleigh is cheaper, and much easier constructed than a wagon, and besides there are plenty of farmers which cannot get to market except in winter.

292. If you had only have went a little closer you would have seen that it wasn't her.

293. The improvements must consist, therefore, in reducing its rules to rational and intelligible principles, and thereby to simplify them.

294. If he is entitled to praise for withdrawing the book as soon as his attention was drawn to it, he would have been entitled to more if there was no necessity for its withdrawal.

295. Among the spectators several of the fair sex were conspicuous, and whose smiles always makes such meetings more agreeable.

296. There was, at the time, in the pockets of the jacket a purse and a pair of kid gloves.

297. Alarmed by these reports it was decided to evacuate the fort that night.

298. Macaulay wrote his history with the twofold purpose of clearing the name of the Whigs from the charges made by Hume, and to set forth the real life of the English people.

299. If the patent has issued in error, or that the Commissioner has been misled, or for other good cause, the Court of Chancery has power to declare such patent void.

300. The Detroit University is open to all who desire a thorough medical education, of either sex.

301. The University has for the special benefit of their students enlisted an able corps of lecturers.

302. Intending matriculants are referred to the Registrar, Professor Siggins, who will give each all instructions and information desired to fully acquaint them with the requirements.

303. It is one of the journals which, while the last administration was in power, shouted itself hoarse in pointing out the iniquity of Mr. M. and the Liberals in general.

304. The University will furnish scholarship certificates for one hundred and fifteen dollars that will entitle its beneficiary to a full course of lectures and instruction.

305. The fee must be paid in advance to the Treasurer, who will enter the name, and give each a ticket that will entitle the holder to, etc.

306. Diseases of the mouth and its contiguous parts will receive its due attention.

307. This will afford a fine means of determining the diagnostic conditions, and to observe the sanative effects of the remedies given.

308. He must possess the knowledge of a three years' course of instruction, as is taught in the University.

309. No one could choose his remedy from the botanical museum around him unless he first becomes acquainted with botanical forms.

310. The University will incorporate in its curriculum of study recognized standard medical, surgical, and scientific authority, as is endorsed by the best schools in America and Europe, and open their doors to all who, etc.

311. The congregation were well repaid by the impressive sermon and the marvellous singing of the choir, in which the ladies predominate, and some of them are unequalled for vocal powers in any other church in the city.

312. The choice being left to the Trustees whether to make the change or not has created a good deal of confusion.

313. Under its influence we do things which we would be sorry to do otherwise.

314. Having received notice to vacate our present premises, and in order to do so, we have decided to get rid of, etc.

315. A man who had been crucified, and risen again, was the centre of their hope, their joy, their affection, their confidence.

316. I cannot make Crito believe that I am the same Socrates who have been talking and conducting the argument; he fancies that I am the other Socrates whom, etc.

317. When he leaves his own state he becomes not only unjust but also displays an ignorance surprising in any educated American.

318. My criticism of the report should have called for gratitude from the committee and the press which published it rather than exciting animosity toward the objector.

319. A. B. begs to announce that he has purchased from C. D. his entire stock and will continue the business at the old stand. Having bought the goods for cash, and as I intend to sell for cash, I will be in a position to offer bargains to my customers.

320. Any man or woman that once buys anything from us are sure to become regular customers.
321. You can omit the names of any whom you know will not be present at it.
322. Our Board has set a good example by dealing in a liberal spirit with the teachers in their employ.
323. I came to the conclusion that the first time I would see them I would thoroughly examine them.
324. I have examined G.'s Revised and Improved System of Penmanship, and I shall advise all the pupils of this school to purchase them only.
325. The worthy Principal, with his staff of able assistants, are well deserving the compliments paid them.
326. Mr. M. refused, and stated that he was going back to C., in the most peremptory manner.
327. It is well understood that five men can transact business just as satisfactorily, and certainly more expeditiously, than forty or fifty.
328. A majority of our Third Class Teachers, after having taught for three years, are unable to obtain a Second Class Certificate, and in consequence of which are compelled to quit the profession.
329. This is one of the few subjects that seems to be thoroughly taught in our schools.
330. Nothing can justify his resort to it so frequently.
331. Nor do I, either in or out of Cambridge, know any one with whom I can converse more pleasantly, or would prefer as my companion.
332. Some Jews in Hungary are accused of having murdered a Christian girl and using her blood to mix with their Passover bread.
333. I would not have thought that he would be so simple as to have believed such a story.
334. Another artist has been engaged of equally high reputation to finish the work.

335. It is so prepared that a patient can take it without disgust until they are permanently benefited.

336. The State has a right to see that parents should so manage their children that they should not become a burden on it.

337. We would advise you to consult your physician about it, as they are our special agents in promoting the sale.

338. A full description, it will be remembered, was given in our last Saturday's issue, of this remarkable structure.

339. And thence dislike, disgust, or cold indifference rise.

340. The mechanical work was executed in Canada, and is pronounced by the most competent judges superior to the rival series manufactured abroad.

341. Any one intending to use Portland cement this fall it would be to their advantage to call and see me at once.

342. Every picture is guaranteed to be the work of the popular artists whose name they bear.

343. A public meeting will be held on Monday evening, at which Mr. A. will address the electors, in addition to several other gentleman.

344. Whatever sprightly juice or tasteful food
On the green bosom of this earth are found.

345. Chinese kites are made like big bats, butterflies, owls, hawks, and other birds.

346. Yet oft in holy writ we see
Even such weak minister as me
May the opposer bruise.

347. We are glad to see this effort made to popularize the writings of Philip Massinger, a man whose taste was purer, and diction finer, than most of his contemporaries.

348. They intend holding a parlor concert at the residence of Mr. J. T., who has the largest in town, and is admirably adapted for the purpose.

349. Resolved: That the Council desires to express its sense of the great loss the town has sustained by his death, and as a mark of respect for his memory do now adjourn.

350. That the Senate, at this its first meeting since his death, record their sorrow at the loss the province has sustained.

351. The undersigned being desirous to clear off the balance of his stock of summer goods in order to make room for my steady increasing business will offer the whole of my stock in such lots as may suit intending purchasers, and at such prices that cannot be approached by any in the town.

352. Yet the vaguest notions prevail as to the amount of this waste, even by those who have paid attention to the subject.

353. If there was any penalty for such conduct we might have better books.

354. The whole chapter on temperance looks as if after being put in type it was shaken in a bag, and then the impression was made.

355. Mr. G. perhaps prefers this sound, though none of the dictionary makers do, or any one who speaks English correctly.

356. The medical profession are already doing more than ought to be expected of its members.

357. The teachers should endeavor to repress the practice of throwing stones as far as possible.

358. I look forward to a time when every new dress will require a pattern, especially when made up at home, and that more taste and economy will be inculcated by this home practice.

359. In answer to it Neptune sent a bull from the sea, by which the horses of Hippolytus were terrified, ran away, and killed their master.

Part III.

SPELLING AND PUNCTUATION.

SPELLING.

It would be inappropriate to insert here a number of exercises in spelling. Such exercises belong rather to work in the grammar school or in the earlier years of the high school than to that of students preparing definitely for college. It is a matter of experience, however, that many even of the candidates at the entrance examinations still spell atrociously, as the following sentences, taken word for word and letter for letter from rejected papers, will show. The words misspelled in them may be by chance just the words which the student himself has difficulty with. If that be the case, so much the better; usually, however, each pupil has his own particular set of blunders, which he must learn to avoid by his own experience. To that end he should be instructed to keep for himself a list of the words he misspells, drilling himself on them until he is sure that he can by no possibility repeat his errors. Good thumb-rules for spelling, if such are needed, can be found in Bigelow's *Handbook of Punctuation*, pp. 71–76.

Words Misspelled.

EXERCISE XXIX.

1. In reading Thackery's English Humorists I was perhaps most interested in the author's account of Jonathan Swift.

2. One of my "conditions" was English Grammer.

3. There one day she saw a poor dieing old man — it was Gabriel.

4. All the inhabittanse of the villiage were driven to the beach and carried to the ships. Families and friends were seperated.

5. My reading, for the last few years, has been mostly historical; principaly upon the War of 1812, between the United States and Great Britian.

6. Two years ago I studdied Harveys English grammar at Lawrenceville New Jersey.

7. It is a question in my mind weather I like his Addison better than his Congreve.

8. They looked for each other for years and finaly met in central United States.

9. He has pictured his moral character with the same bright colors and with the same irrisistable humor.

10. Mr. R. was a very severe master on the subject of grammer and our lessons were often long and tedious. We read and analized "Grey's Elegy" and Peace and War. We were also obliged to commit Grey's Elegy to memory and if Mr. R. gave us one word from any versc we would have to analize or parce that verse.

11. A knowledge of english is always to one's benefit, it enables him to speak correctly and also gives him a knowledge of history which is desireable.

12. Being compelled to write esseys in my former school, I looked upon it as a task rather than a pleasure.

13. She, loosing track of him, spends her time nursing those wounded in the battles.

14. Thus the homes of the Acadians were blotted out of thier view.

15. Gabriel went to the west, where Evangeline followed him but only to be dissapointed.

16. The farmer vainly tryed to cheer him as they sat and smoked.

17. She travells all over the country but he is always beyond; untill she is old and careworn she keeps up the search, and at last finds him in a hospital on his death bed.

18. She knew him at once, though wrinkled by age and emaciated by fever.

19. To my mind Brutus seems to deserve to be called the best caracter in Julius Caesar, more than any other.

20. Gabriel and Evangeline are seperated, and as the ships landed in different ports of the English colonies, there now commences the sadest part of our story.

21. When I saw the examination paper last June, you can immagin my feelings.

22. They were berried side by side in the little church yard near by.

23. The preparation of exercises in parsing and analizing and the learning off rules and definitions were required by the school.

24. An expedition was sent against them, and the peaceful farmers were transfered to the English ships and thence distributed among the colonies.

25. But that morning Caesar thought he would not go to the Senet house because the omens were unfavorable but Brutus, who was Caesars friend, and who is the principal character of the play, purswades him to go.

26. Brutus, Cassius and some other men thought he would take the power if he can get it. So they conspire against him, and choos the Ides of March to assassanate him.

27. Upon my request he made some selections from it for my immeadiate use.

28. In the last class of the grammer school I studied the eliments of English grammer, parceing sentences and words and writing compositions.

29. The last year in the school I studied English Literature taking part of the principle authors.

30. He expressed as his oppinion that the English had no good intension in coming, and stated that the men were to be summoned to the village church on the following day.

At noon on the next day the church bell towled and Basil, Benedict, and Gabriel went to the church. The doors being bared, and guarded by soldiers, the commander of the English arose, and told them that they were prisoners of war, and that they were to be distributed among the English colonies.

31. The eliments of style are, words, sentances, paragraphs, and whole compositions.

32. But I never recieved your letter.

PUNCTUATION.

The main principles of punctuation are best learned from Bigelow's *Handbook of Punctuation*, a short treatise, equally valuable as a text-book and as a book of reference. The management of the marks of punctuation is largely a matter of common-sense. The system is simple and flexible and can easily be mastered by any one who keeps in mind the function of each of the marks of punctuation.[1]

EXERCISE XXX.

Punctuate the following passages:—

1. As soon as a child has learned to form his letters without trouble his attention should be called not only to spelling punctuation and grammar but also to the choice of words and to the construction of simple sentences and he should be obliged to master every point that comes under the head of correctness In this matter the instructor should not spare himself should resist the temptation to spend time on the curiosities of language or in the pleasant places of literature rather than in the correction of petty errors and should constantly bear in mind that unless petty errors are corrected at the beginning there is danger that they never will be.

Knowledge of conventional rules is I am told of incomparably less importance than the possession of those qualities in style which give a man the power to influence other men's thoughts and actions but this remark true enough in itself has no application to children In English as in everything else children must be taught the rudiments first. To omit them altogether or to postpone them too long is to act like a student in architecture who should pay no attention to questions of construction or should take them up for the first time after he had acquainted himself with the mysteries of the so-called Queen Anne style Such an architect might forget

[1] The period, for instance, is a full stop, and shows that the sentence structure is logically and grammatically complete. The semicolon marks a main, and the comma a lesser, joint in the sentence. The colon is always a mark of specification. The function of the other points is obvious.

to leave room in his plan for a necessary staircase and his chimneys would surely smoke Such a writer would be lame in his grammar and would probably not know how to spell or to punctuate[1]

2. Not that I would in pursuance of Mr Benjamin F Butlers advice replace the spelling book in its former commanding position in the schools and compel boys and girls to learn long lists of words which they would have no occasion to use but every one should be able to spell the words that are often on his lips or often under his eye in the books he studies or reads Not that I would perplex a young mind with punctuation as a system or with nice questions between semicolons and colons but every one should at an early age be taught the difference between the period and the comma and the principal functions of each every one should be taught too the general principle that a point serves as a guide to the construction and through the construction to the meaning of a sentence[2]

3. Several hours judiciously used should suffice to teach an intelligent boy the few points of grammar which it is most necessary to know for the assertion that English is a grammarless tongue though an exaggeration and a harmful one if understood literally has a basis in the fact that the changes of form in English words are very few and that the rules of syntax are far simpler in our language than in most others A few nouns form peculiar plurals a few verbs peculiar participles and a very few verbs are peculiar throughout but most of these exceptions occur in words which everybody uses so often that it is easy to learn the correct forms A similar remark may be made concerning who and whom I and me and the other pronouns Let a boy be taught to use his pronouns correctly and to place them where there can be no doubt as to their antecedents to couple singulars with singulars and plurals with plurals to observe the distinction between shall and will to put verbs referring to the same time in the same tense not to destroy

[1] A. S. Hill, *Our English*, p. 17. [2] *Ibid.* p. 19.

a negative by doubling it not to interpolate adverbs between the two parts of the infinitive as in to blindly follow to so say a common error to insert every word that is essential to the grammar and to strike out every word that is superfluous let a boy be taught these things and he will be far on the road to correct expression[1]

4. You mean Mr St George isnt he delightful

Paul Overt looked at her a moment

Alas I dont know him I only admire him at a distance

Oh you must know him he wants so to talk to you rejoined Miss Fancourt who evidently had the habit of saying the things that by her quick calculation would give people pleasure

I shouldnt have supposed he knew anything about me Paul said smiling

He does then everything And if he didnt I should be able to tell him

To tell him everything

You talk just like the people in your book the girl exclaimed

Then they must all talk alike

Well it must be so difficult Mr. St George tells me it is terribly Ive tried too and I find it so Ive tried to write a novel

Mr St George oughtnt to discourage you said Paul Overt

You do much more when you wear that expression

Well after all why try to be an artist the young man went on Its so poor so poor

I dont know what you mean said Marian Fancourt looking grave

I mean as compared with being a person of action as living your works

But what is art but a life if it be real asked the girl I think its the only one everything else is so clumsy Paul Overt laughed and she continued Its so interesting meeting so many celebrated people

So I should think but surely it isnt new to you

Why I have never seen any one any one living always in Asia

---

[1] A. S. Hill, *Our English*, p. 22.

But doesnt Asia swarm with personages Havent you administered provinces in India and had captive rajahs and tributary princes chained to your car

I was with my father after I left school to go out there It was delightful being with him we are alone together in the world he and I but there was none of the society I liked best One never never heard of a picture never of a book except bad ones

Never of a picture Why wasnt all life a picture

Miss Fancourt looked over the delightful place where they sat Nothing to compare with this I adore England she exclaimed

Ah of course I dont deny that we must do something with it yet

It hasnt been touched really said the girl

Did Henry St George say that[1]

5. Among English books that I have put under contribution I may mention Kloses Memoirs of Prince Charles Edward Stuart Colburn 1845 Ewalds Life and Times of Prince Charles Stuart Chapman and Hall 1875 and Sir Horace Manns Letters to Walpole edited by Dr Doran A review variously attributed to Lockhart and to Dennistoun in the Quarterly for 1847 has been all the more useful to me as I have been unable to procure writing in Italy the Tales of a Century of which that paper gives a masterly account[2]

EXERCISE XXXI.

Correct the punctuation in the following extracts:—

1. Miles Standish, although an authentic historical character, is more often thought of; and perhaps better known, through the writings of our poet; countryman; Longfellow, who, with a masters grace so beautifully depicts to the imagination, the character, feelings, duties and passions; of this plain and rigid soldier, colonist, and warrior.

---

[1] Henry James, *The Lesson of the Master*, p. 16.

[2] Vernon Lee, *The Countess of Albany*, p. ix.

He was not particularly noted for the beauty of his countenance: which was bronzed, and scarred; by years of toil and exposure; both in Old England, and the new colony. Standish was a short, thick set, muscular man. A man of action and deeds, not words, ready to brave danger in defence of the colony, and even willing to do his share of the work, and duty; both as citizen, and soldier. He was in his element as commander of the embryo army of the new colony: and but waited a chance, to strike terror, to any prowling, or molesting savage. Plain in manner, life and dress, Standish was still human, he had an eye for the beautiful, and a dread, of the solitary: individual companionship was not what he desired. Being a man of war, rigid and stern; his feelings were not always expressed in words, others might talk, Standish would plan, and carry out. Still, as human beings are all bound to have their disappointments, and "the best laid schemes of mice and men," some times fail to accomplish all they desire, So was the plan of this sincere and earnest man. A man of cold calculation and sound judgment: based on hope, and the ability of others, as instruments to effect an end. Thus being reticent and feeling himself personally unable to properly demean himself; he rests the power of attorney in another.

2. Too well, did Cassius know what would be the effect of an attack on the forces of Mark Antony and Octavius Cæsar. Yet, rather than displease Brutus, he had agreed that on the following day the attack should be made at Philippi.

During the first part of the march there had been several signs which portended good to the army of Brutus, — eagles had hovered above his standards and taken food from the soldiers' hands, but as his men neared the battle field the good signs — changed to bad, — instead of the eagles, ravens and cadaverous birds flew over their heads.

Philippi was reached. After a short parley between the generals, a charge was ordered, Cassius opposing Octavius Cæsar while Brutus attacked Mark Antony.

The battle was short and sharp, Cassius was soon overcome and routed. In his great despair and sorrow at losing the battle Cassius ran against his own sword and so died. Meanwhile Brutus although more successful than Cassius, had lost his battle also, and on hearing that his best general, Cassius, had killed himself he too ran against his sword.

And thus the great conspiracy which had cost the world one of the greatest men who ever lived, came to an end.

3. Years ago, upon one of the towers of Granada, was the bronze figure of a horseman, with uplifted lance.

When the king of this country was young, he had been always at war with his neighbors, and when old age overcame him, and the warlike spirit within him had died out, he was greatly worried, because his neighbors would not let him live in peace and quietude.

It was at this time, that an old man came one day before him. The king, after conversing with him, found that he was an Arabian astrologer, and had learned the art of magic in Egypt.

The king told him of his troubles, and the astrologer promised to help him. Accordingly he placed on the top of a tower, overlooking the surrounding country, the figure of the horseman; and on a table, in the room of the tower, he placed wooden figures of men, and horses, in representation of an army. At whatever point danger threatened the bronze figure turned, and pointed its lance. By means of this the king's enemies were not able to surprise him.

One day the figure turned and levelled its lance, and following the direction indicated by the lance, the king's soldiers found a beautiful woman, whom they brought to the city. The king fell madly in love with her, and the astrologer promised to build him, an invisible palace, wherein he, and his beloved, might live in seclusion.

The palace was built, and the astrologer named as his reward, the first beast of burden, and it's load, that should enter the palace gate.

On the appointed day, the king went to look at his palace, and the woman riding ahead, was the first to enter the gate.

Upon this, the astrologer claimed his reward, whereupon the king grew furious; but the astrologer, grasping the bridle of the ass, sank with the woman, into the ground.

The king spent many days, in digging, and searching for them, but in vain, for he never again saw either.

Use of Capitals.

EXERCISE XXXII.

Change small letters to capitals wherever they are necessary. Give your reasons. For rules see Bigelow, "Handbook of Punctuation," Chapter VII.

1. "who were the founders of our race? working backwards, up the stream of national descent, we come to the great influx of norman people, norman words, norman ways; and we stop to reckon with this fact in the development of english life. a very brief study, a few minutes of consideration, assure us that here are no founders of England, but only generous contributors; immigrants we may call them, who brought along valuable property, and furnished us with some new and desirable elements of civilization. again, and for still stronger reasons, we reach the same conclusion with regard to that earlier conquest of england by the northmen. the danes gave us a few words, — the common vocable 'are', for example, — a few customs, a few laws; and that is the whole story. it lies, therefore, between the celts, the people whom cæsar found in his britain, and the germanic invaders and conquerors who seized upon the island when the roman legions were withdrawn. of these two claimants, the latter race is recognized by history and criticism as furnishing the real foundation of our national life. true, there is more or less opposition in the matter of actual descent. we are germanic in our institutions, concedes professor huxley; but the race itself is at least half celtic in its blood. 'not one half', mr. grant allen is inclined to think, 'of the population of the british isles is really of teutonic

descent;' and he carries the battle into still remoter territory when he concedes our language to germanic origins, but claims our literature, especially the imagination displayed in it, for celtic influences. furthermore, the greatest of our critics in literary matters, the late matthew arnold, has broken a lance for this celtic influence in our national development, and is half inclined to answer the question, 'what is england?' by saying, 'a vast obscure cymric basis with a vast visible germanic superstructure.' in particular, arnold attributes so high a quality of our literature as its humor — and what quality is so peculiarly its own, so triumphantly its own? — to the dash of celtic impulse and fancy, clashing with our germanism."[1]

2. "But it was not the chancellor of the exchequer and mr. morley only who made this appeal to the universities. in the january number of the *quarterly review* for 1887, many, . . whose distinction in letters justly entitled them to speak with authority on this matter, have expressed precisely similar views on the subject of the relation of philology to literature. . . . among the names of those who supported this movement are to be found the names of the archbishop of canterbury, cardinal manning, the bishop of london, mr. gladstone, lord lytton, professor jowett, matthew arnold, professor huxley, mr. froude, sir theodore martin, and many others."[2]

EXERCISE XXXIII.

In the following sentences use capitals wherever they are necessary. Give your reason in each case

1. I was prepared at the detroit high school two years ago and I have had no instruction since then except by myself.

2. The first year I studied english grammar, the second year shakspere's plays, julius cæsar, merchant of venice, and scott's marmion.

---

[1] Gummere, *Germanic Origins*, p. 1.

[2] Collins, *The Study of English Literature*, p. vi.

3. The next spring miles standish, captain of the colony of plymouth, marched with his little company west against the hostile indians.

4. Of all the governors this state has ever had governor smith is the most popular.

5. The college of the city of new york is situated in the city of new york.

6. The west and the east are more alike in point of dialect than the north and the south.

7. The title of the novel, which ran as a serial in scribner's monthly, is the wrecker.

8. One day there came to Granada an arabian astrologer who told the king a long story about his finding the book of solomon the wise.

9. The english and the french are as different as the chinese and the japanese.

10. His father was a catholic and his mother a scotch presbyterian.

"Bad" Sentences.

A vexatious error not uncommon in the papers of candidates for admission is one which has not a definite name. It consists in running together, as it were, sentences or clauses which would naturally and logically be kept apart by periods or by semicolons, separating them only by commas. In other words, it is the replacing of a "full stop" by a "stop" of lesser magnitude. For instance, the two sentences, "The first thing to consider is the subject of the work. It should not be too broad," becomes, in the hands of the illiterate writer, "The first thing to consider is the subject of the work, it should not be too broad." Too much pains cannot be taken to eradicate this childish error, the presence of which in an examination paper, except as the result of accident, can be taken as an almost infallible test of the student's lack of suitable preparation. After it is certain that a pupil understands thoroughly why this error is an error,—and a bad one,—he should correct the following sentences; afterwards it would be well to notice carefully whether he commits in his own themes or examination papers, without observing it, the same fault which he has been taught to recognize only in the work of his fellows. Not unfrequently that will be found to be the case.

EXERCISE XXXIV.

1. But Standish had his peculiarities, he was very stern and quiet of manner. Longfellow has pictured him very prettily in his

poem, entitled The Courtship of Miles Standish, he sees a girl in which he is very much interested so he sends his faithful friend John to ask her if she would take Miles for her husband, so John went on his errand which was a very bitter one as this fair maiden was the pride of John's heart, well John asked her if she would marry Miles, her answer was, why does he not come himself, then John said, he has no time, that was the "last straw that broke the camel's back" as far as Miles is concerned, but she said John, why dont you ask for yourself, John was horror stricken, he got up and ran home and told Miles the whole story which made Miles so angry that he went off to fight Indians and was killed but not until John had married the fair maiden.

2. Plain in manner, life and dress Standish was still human, he had an eye for the beautiful, a dread of the solitary, individual companionship was not what he desired.

3. Over the hot waste of sand, his horse sinking to his fetlock at every stride, so loaded is he with the war panoply of the age, rides a Knight with head bowed and his eyes half closed, he has ridden since early morn and has not as yet seen a bush or tree where he might rest, and his jaded steed crop a mouthful of leaves.

4. Suddenly he hears a gentle neigh from his horse, raising his head, shading his eyes with his hand, he examines the horizon carefully, and to his joy beholds the waving tops of palm trees.

5. Neither speak for there is no occasion, both know what is bound to come. The Arab begins the battle by riding in a circle, first quite a distance, around the Christian warrior, gradually he narrows his circle.

6. But it is useless for the shield of the Knight is always before him and seems to cover his whole body the Arab comes nearer and nearer each time when suddenly the Knight's arm flies up with a mighty effort and he hurls his mace at his enemy so suddenly is it done, it takes the Arab by surprise and striking him full on his light target which he carries on his arm, hurls him from his horse.

7. He also appears to have been stern and haughty when the occasion required, the reply to Alden after his eventful errand to Priscilla, his haughty bearing in the council of the english when he answers to the message from the indians are examples.

8. He explained to the delighted monarch, that when the horseman on the tower knew of the approach of enemies he would point in their direction and the little soldiery on the board, that were in the direction indicated, would begin to move, then all the king had to do was, if he desired blood to stir up the soldiers with the point of the lance, if not, with the butt.

9. Miles Standish was a far-sighted, clear-headed man, he was honest in his way though very quick tempered, he was a man to quickly forgive if he saw a mistake.

10. The astrologer promised to relieve him of his trouble, he accordingly commenced by ordering to be built, a watch tower near one of the mountain passes.

PART IV

STYLE.

MISUSED WORDS.

I. — CONFOUNDING WORDS OF SIMILAR SOUND OR ORIGIN.

EXERCISE XXXV.

1. His story does seem rather incredulous.
2. I have been creditably informed that such is the case.
3. It would be impossible to predicate the result of such a contest.[1]
4. He found them in want of the commonest necessities of life.
5. His spirits do not seem to have been high, but they were singularly equitable.
6. Be careful not to confuse these two words.
7. When he reached the age of eighteen, his father was very glad to except for him a clerkship in the East India Co.
8. He stands high in the list of fictitious writers.
9. He agreed not to offer a fictitious opposition to the government.
10. The bodies were so disfigured as to render their identity difficult.
11. He was doomed to expatiate his crimes on the gallows.
12. I hope you may succeed in convicting him of his error.

---

[1] "*Predicate* (Lat. *praedĭcāre*, 'to publish, state,' from *prae*, 'before, publicly,' and *dĭcāre*, 'to say') is a different word from *predict* (Lat. *praedīcĕre*, 'to foretell,' from *prae*, 'beforehand,' and *dīcĕre*, 'to tell')." — Hodgson, p. 51.

13. How will the new regulations effect your school?

14. We proposed to go to-morrow, but I fear the rain will prevent us.[1]

15. He depreciated the attempt made by the last speaker to excite a prejudice against the company.

16. He was allowed to pursue his ordinary avocation in peace.[2]

17. The observation of these simple rules would have prevented all difficulty.

18. When he first meets Silas he is a young weaver in Lantern Yard, happy in his avocation and apparently imbued with a true religious spirit.

Wrong Forms of Words.

19. I enthuse with the achievements of his heroes, and fall in love with his heroines.

20. He then pled his case, although without avail, before a still higher court.[3]

21. That he had such extraordinary talents is by no means proven.[4]

22. He was looked upon as a progedy of learning.

23. He went to see the tradegy of *Macbeth* played.

24. He seemed to regard it as a clever stragetic movement.

25. He recommended it to us as an excellent dentrifice.

---

1 "No two terms are more commonly confounded than Purpose and Propose; but the former denotes a settled, the latter a contingent state of mind. I *propose* to do something, if I have not yet made up my mind. I *purpose* when I *have* made up my mind. Yet the words Purpose and Propose might often be used indifferently, provided it be remembered that they express different aspects of the same thing. I *purpose* to do a thing when I have formed a practical intention to do it. I *propose* to do it when I recognize it as a design which I shall carry out, provided that nothing occurs to hinder or deter me." — Smith's *Synonyms Discriminated.*

2 *Avocation.* "That which calls one away from one's proper business; a subordinate or occasional occupation; a diversion or distraction. A person's regular business or occupation; vocation; calling. [An improper though common use of the word.] " — *The Century Dictionary.*

3 The preterite and past participle of *plead* is *pleaded,* not *plead* (*pled*).

4 "An improper form of the past participle *proved,* 'lately growing in frequency, by imitation of the Scotch use in "not proven."' " — *The Century Dictionary.*

26. A suppositious copy. A box of blackening. I had as leave.

27. An unhappy casuality. A serious grieviance. Illy repaid for it.

28. We had exceptionably good opportunities.

29. He wiped away the prespiration.

30. I remain, yours respectively.

31. He was reading about a hippotamus.

II.—Confounding Synonyms or Words of Related Meaning.

EXERCISE XXXVI.

1. He seemed disposed to question the veracity of my statements.

2. He was not conscious of what had been done in his absence.[1]

3. Tomatoes are said to be very healthy food.[2]

4. Silas is said to be a typical English weaver, who loves his loom and takes an interest in everything transpiring around him.

5. Did you send a verbal or a written message?[3]

6. In that way you will be more liable to get at the truth.

7. I don't propose to let you escape so easily.

8. After a considerable interval had transpired, he returned to the office.

9. Her future life is said to have been virtuous and irreproachable.

---

[1] "*Aware, Conscious. Aware* refers commonly to objects of perception outside of ourselves; *conscious*, to objects of perception within us: as, to become *aware* of the presence of a stranger; to be quite *aware* of the danger of one's situation; to become *conscious* of a pain in one's eye. *Aware* indicates perception without feeling; *conscious*, generally recognition with some degree of feeling."—*The Century Dictionary*, p. 1203, v. 2.

[2] "A distinction between *healthy* and *healthful* is nearly established. *Healthy* is applicable to the condition of body or mind; *healthful* to that which produces health."—*The Century Dictionary*, p. 2754, v. 3.

[3] *Oral* and *Verbal. Oral:* expressed in spoken words; *verbal:* properly, relating to or concerned with words only; improperly confounded with *oral*. For excellent examples of the correct and the erroneous use of *verbal* see Hodgson's *Errors in the Use of English*, pp. 66–68.

10. I never saw such a quantity of sheep at a show before.

11. Such carelessness is calculated to leave a very unfavorable impression on the minds of the examiners.[1]

12. Had this been done, their object would doubtless have been successful.

13. The enormity of the cost of the proposed tunnel seemed to startle him.

14. The discovery of the telescope rendered it a comparatively easy task.

15. You will be very apt to find him in the billiard room.[2]

16. The whole family enjoy a rather bad reputation and very poor health.

17. The death of the veteran journalist is hourly anticipated.

18. There is no doubt that his death was hastened by the blows administered by the policeman.[3]

19. The conscience of the purity and disinterestedness of his motives consoled him for his defeat.

20. I did not hear his reply to your question.

21. There is a crack running down the centre of the wall.

---

1 *Calculate.* Used locally in the United States, outside of its strictly mathematical meaning, as equivalent to *think* or *guess*, or to *purpose*, *intend*, or *design*. "You are wrong there, I calculate." "He calculates to do it."

2 *Apt, Likely, Liable.* "*Apt*, when used in the sense of persons, indicates physical tendency or inward inclination: as, *apt* to catch cold; *apt* to neglect work; when used of things, it similarly indicates natural tendency: as, *apt* to mold.

"*Likely* may suggest the same idea: as, he is *likely* to do it; it is *likely* to rust; or it may express mere external probability or chance: as, he is *likely* to come at any moment.

"*Liable* in this connection is properly used only of exposure to evil, being practically equivalent to exposed, or exposed to the danger of: as, *liable* to be hurt, that is, exposed to the danger of being hurt: in such use it does not express probability or tendency, but merely the possibility of exposure or risk. *Subject* expresses what is likely to happen to a person or thing, and occasionally does happen. *Liable* to disease and *subject* to disease thus convey different ideas. The things to which we are *liable* are determined more by accident or circumstance; the things to which we are *subject* are determined by nature and constitution. *Apt* to be suddenly ill; *liable*, but not *likely*, to die before the physician arrives; *subject* to attacks of epilepsy." — *The Century Dictionary.*

3 Consult the dictionary on this point.

III.—MISCELLANEOUS EXAMPLES OF MISUSED WORDS.

EXERCISE XXXVII.

1. You want to be very careful to explain this point clearly.
2. He agreed to return it inside of ten days.
3. By so doing he imputes the veracity of the secretary.
4. The infallible result will be to discourage them.
5. My interests are synonymous with yours.
6. It is one of the worst crops we have ever experienced.
7. The troops were terribly decimated by the fire.[1]
8. Such conduct deserves the most condign punishment.[2]
9. He may take his choice of the three alternatives.[3]
10. We have no desire to deteriorate from its merit.
11. Unfortunately cleverness will not condone for inaccuracy.[4]
12. It was with difficulty that he eliminated the desired information.[5]
13. It is published at the very limited rate of fifty cents a year.
14. I knew he was ill, but did not think he was dangerous.
15. Unluckily a nail had made a capacious rent in the garment.
16. In this way the requisitions of grammar would be satisfied, and those of euphony too.
17. Though small, the book contains a host of useful information.
18. For many years deceased was a native of the County of Huron.

---

[1] *Decimate.* Literally, to take the tenth part of or from, but loosely and improperly, to destroy a great but indefinite number or proportion of.

[2] *Condign.* Suitable, deserved, merited; not necessarily *severe*, though frequently used in that sense by careless writers.

[3] *Alternative.* "A choice between *two* things; a possibility of one of *two* things. One of the two things of which either is possible or may be chosen."—*The Century Dictionary.*

[4] Consult the dictionary on this point.

[5] *Eliminate.* Properly used in its mathematical sense or with a similar figurative meaning; without justification, though not uncommon, as a synonym of *deduce* or *elicit.*

19. Some of these remarks aggravated him almost beyond the bounds of endurance.[1]

20. I am not liable to meet with any such good fortune.[2]

21. The climax of all his hopes was reached when he was appointed lieutenant in the artillery.[3]

22. I would not demean myself by accepting any offer of that sort which you could make.[4]

23. He is about the nicest man I ever saw — so good-natured.[5]

24. There is another party coming to-night, but he will leave early in the morning.[6]

---

[1] *Aggravate.* (1) "To make more grave or heavy; increase the weight or pressure; intensify, as anything evil, disorderly, or troublesome: as, to *aggravate* guilt or crime, the evils or annoyances of life." (2) "To provoke, irritate, tease. [Colloquial.]" — *The Century Dictionary.*

[2] See p. 85, note 2.

[3] *Climax.* Frequently, and not without authority, used in the sense of *acme.*

[4] *Demean.* "Reflexively, to behave; carry; conduct. To debase; lower; lower the dignity or standing of; bemean. [This is in origin a misuse of *demean* by association with the adjective *mean.* Being thus illegitimate in origin and inconvenient in use, from its tendency to be confused with *demean* in its proper sense, the word is avoided by scrupulous writers.]" — *The Century Dictionary.*

[5] *Nice.* "Archdeacon Hare remarks of the use, or rather misuse, of this word: 'That stupid vulgarism by which we use the word *nice* to denote almost every mode of approbation, for almost every variety of quality, and, from sheer poverty of thought, or fear of saying anything definite, wrap up everything indiscriminately in this characterless domino, speaking at the same breath of a *nice* cheese-cake, a *nice* tragedy, a *nice* sermon, a *nice* day, a *nice* country, as if a universal deluge of *niaiserie* — for *nice* seems originally to have been only *niais* — had whelmed the whole island.' *Nice* is as good a word as any other in its place, but its place is not everywhere. We talk very properly about a *nice* distinction, a *nice* discrimination, a *nice* calculation, a *nice* point, and about a person's being *nice*, and over-*nice*, and the like; but we certainly ought not to talk about 'Othello's being a *nice* tragedy, about Salvini's being a *nice* actor, or New York bay's being a *nice* harbor." — *The Verbalist.*

On the other hand, *The Century Dictionary* states the case less dogmatically when it gives as a later, acquired meaning of *nice:* "Pleasing or agreeable in general. (*a*) Elegant or tasteful; pleasing; pleasant: often used with some implication of contempt. (*b*) Agreeable; pleasant; good: applied to persons. [Colloquial.]

"[*Nice* in this sense is very common in colloquial use as a general epithet of approbation applicable to anything that pleases.]"

[6] *Party.* Besides its usual meanings, *party* is sometimes used in the sense of: "A person; a particular person, as distinct from and opposed to any other; a

25. Quite a number of us were walking the other day when we saw quite a few (*i.e.* a good many) quails on the other side of the fence. They were all quite (*i.e.* moderately) large.[1]

26. It's real good of you to want me to stop over night, but I am afraid it will storm to-morrow.[2]

CHOICE OF WORDS.

EXERCISE XXXVIII.

Which of the italicized words or expressions in the following sentences are preferable?

1. The letter was addressed to the *Reverent* (*Reverend*) Mr. Smith.
2. The children behaved in a very *reverent* (*reverend*) manner.
3. I would have gone if it had been *ever* (*never*) so stormy.[3]
4. He ought to be put in a *straight* (*strait*) jacket.
5. He set before them a most *luxurious* (*luxuriant*) banquet.

---

person under special consideration; a person in general; an individual: as, an old *party* of my acquaintance. [Now only vulgar.] 'He's a genteel-looking party. I wonder if he belongs to Sotor, King & Co., of New York?'—C. D. WARNER." — *The Century Dictionary.*

[1] *Quite.* Properly used in the sense of "completely," "wholly"; improperly used colloquially to mean "to a considerable extent or degree": as, *quite* warm, *quite* a few.

[2] *Real.* "This adjective is often vulgarly used in the sense of the adverb *very*: thus, *real* nice, *real* angry, *real* 'cute,' and so on." — *The Verbalist.*

Stop. "To *stop* means to cease to go forward, to leave off; and to *stay* means to abide, to tarry, to dwell, to sojourn. We *stay*, not *stop*, at home, at a hotel, or with a friend, as the case may be." — *The Verbalist.*

Storm. "Many persons indulge in a careless use of this word, using it when they mean to say simply that it rains or snows. To a *storm* a violent commotion of the atmosphere is indispensable. A very high wind constitutes a storm, though it be dry." — *The Verbalist.*

[3] "This expression (*ever so*) has been substituted, from a notion of logical propriety, for *never so*, which in literary use appears to be much older, and still occurs as an archaism." — Murray's *A New English Dictionary*, under *Ever*, 9, *b*.

6. What method of *proceeding* (*procedure*) would you adopt in such a case?

7. I heard it from our *mutual* (*common*) friend.

8. Were your instructions *oral* (*verbal*) or written?

9. He soon acquired the *custom* (*habit*) of using opium.

10. He insisted on the prompt *observance* (*observation*) of the regulations.

11. Don't leave any more than you *can* (*can't*) help.

12. The goods are to be sold *at* (*by*) auction to-morrow.

13. He professed great sympathy *with* (*for*) them.

14. The counter was covered with a *various* (*varied*) assortment of cards.

15. His face assumed a *deadly* (*deathly*) paleness.

16. To inflict *corporeal* (*corporal*) punishment.

17. To preserve it as a *relict* (*relic*) of his school life.

18. He was exposed to *continual* (*continuous*) interruptions.

19. The facts are just the *converse* (*reverse*) of what he states.

20. To have been guilty of a long course of *deception* (*deceit*).

21. To write *under* (*over*) the signature of, etc.

22. He has no *relations* (*relatives*) in this country.

23. They had acquired large *tracts* (*tracks*) of land.

24. Probably he belongs to a theatrical *troop* (*troupe*).

25. The *first three* (the *three first*) names on the list.

EXERCISE XXXIX.

Improve the following sentences by substituting correct forms of expression for such as are wrong or of doubtful propriety.[1]

1. You had no call to leave it within his reach.
2. He wasn't injured any as far as I could see.
3. Do you mind what I told you last day?
4. He as good as offered to take them both.
5. He got left behind by the train this morning.

---

[1] The pupil should understand that an expression may be colloquial without being rhetorically improper.

6. Don't let on that you see him.
7. He wasn't quite so bad when we left.
8. He was noways to blame for the accident.
9. He waited a little bit to see what he would do.
10. He waited quite a spell in the hope of seeing them.
11. It is rather better than a month since he left.
12. He seemed to be thoroughly posted on such matters.
13. I thought it a pity of him to have to go alone.
14. He seemed to feel rather put out about it.
15. It isn't above a fortnight since we saw him.
16. I need a new brush the worst way.
17. He is in a worse fix now than he ever was.
18. Are you done with the ruler now?
19. He never named the matter to us.
20. He promised to come right away.
21. He will blame it on you.
22. He took me apart to tell me the news.
23. What could have possessed him to do it?
24. He seemed bound to make the attempt.
25. Here they come, and Smith among the rest.
26. It is funny that you did not see him.
27. He was necessitated to apply to them.

EXERCISE XL.

Distinguish between the following.

1. He was unable to construe (construct) a sentence.
2. That is a very ingenious (ingenuous) explanation.
3. Divers (diverse) methods of accomplishing it were proposed.
4. He purposed (proposed) to unite the two classes.
5. It may possibly affect (effect) the desired result.
6. He suggested a practical (practicable) method of accomplishing it.
7. He told them to bring (fetch) their books.
8. She failed in her efforts to conciliate (reconcile) them.

9. He spoke contemptuously (contemptibly) of the President.
10. He made three successful (successive) attempts to reach it.
11. He referred (alluded) to it in his sermon.
12. He said he would come to-morrow (on the morrow).
13. He regarded it as a politic (political) scheme.
14. He alone can do it. He can do it alone.
15. I was reading a serial (serious) story.
16. Only one did the deductions. One did the deductions only.
17. She is at least as tall as you (as tall as you at least).
18. They won a decided (decisive) victory.
19. One is very likely (liable) to be deceived.
20. A vacant house. An empty house.
21. The entire outfit. A complete outfit.
22. The victim of a delusion (an illusion).
23. Sanitary (sanatory) measures.
24. He stood motionless (unmoved) (immovable).
25. Endeavored to convince (convict) him.
26. To compare (contrast) the two methods.
27. An Irish emigrant (immigrant).
28. I can't recollect (remember) the formula.
29. An equivocal (ambiguous) answer.
30. A man's capacity (ability).
31. To persuade (convince) a man.
32. An idle (indolent) pupil.
33. A diligent (an industrious) pupil.
34. To have plenty (abundance) of a thing.
35. Elected by a plurality (majority).
36. Childish (child-like) conduct.
37. An ignorant (illiterate) man.
38. Caused by neglect (negligence).
39. Incur hatred (odium).
40. He gave his assent (consent).
41. Transient (transitory) pleasures.
42. To abbreviate. To abridge.
43. He rebuked (reproved) them.

44. To attain (obtain) a thing.
45. To be guilty of dissimulation (hypocrisy).
46. To restore amicable (friendly) relations.
47. Prudent councils (counsels).

EXERCISE XLI.

Express the following in simpler and more natural language.

1. The majority of the residents of the locality.
2. The unmistakable precursor.
3. The extreme felicity.
4. An exceedingly opulent individual.
5. A condition of complete indigence.
6. His customary beverage.
7. Participate in the pecuniary advantages.
8. Encountered an elderly individual.
9. Arrived in close proximity.
10. To lead to the hymeneal altar.
11. Made the recipient of the grateful acknowledgments.
12. An individual evidently identified with the agricultural interests.
13. Proceeded to his residence.
14. The services of the nearest physician were called into requisition.
15. His immortal spirit had quitted its earthly habitation.
16. The conflagration attracted an immense concourse of spectators.
17. To arrest the progress of the devouring element.
18. The assembled populace commenced to evince a disposition to, etc.
19. The unprecedented inclemency of the weather necessitated its postponement.
20. Endeavored to conceal his repugnance.
21. Sustained a fracture of the clavicle.
22. It will in all human probability eventuate in.

23. To institute a comparison between the two.

24. To inaugurate the contest.

25. At the earliest practicable period.

26. In olden times, when the spinning wheel hummed merrily in every household, there would often be found in the secluded districts among the hills, a few mysterious-appearing men, who were always looked upon by the country people with suspicion, especially when one of them were seen trudging over a distant hill with his mysterious bag upon his back, standing out in bold relief against the evening sky.

27. Webster as an orator surpasses, Demosthenes always excepted, every other example known in the annals of time.

Whether we observe that admirable diction; to which the lofty style of Gibbon cannot be compared or stand intranced by the elegant adaptiveness of that noble imagery, unparalleled even by Bacon, we must confess he stands pre-eminent, above all; even as the lofty cedar of Lebanon over-tops the weeping willow of Cyprus.

But what we chiefly admire is the disgust and abhorrence he displays at anything bombastic and superficial.

Can anything be more inspiring than the feelings which prompted this lofty soul to give utterance to that inimitable and crowning stone of oratory, "The First Bunker Hill Oration"? The subject was one well calculated to bring forth all the noble passions surging in the breast of Man.

A few "sons of freedom" had stood up, nerved by all the fires of freedom, against a horde of disciplined warriors, habituated to victory in every land and against every foe, had driven them from the forests of freedom and had declared the "Western World" free, from the shores of the Southern Gulf to the Great Lakes of North America.

In a few years the "two or three millions had augmented to ten million souls," the bird of freedom could fly unchecked from ocean to ocean, the vast and gloomy wilderness had gone down before the sturdy pioneer's axe, and Europe beheld a new Empire, an Empire based on reason, on purity, and on a just regard for every freeman's rights spring from the immense wilderness with the rapidity of the prophet's gourd

It was at this time, just before the immortal Webster withdrew from the political arena; magnanimously withdrawing in favor of his opponent and voluntarily relinquishing all claims to the nomination for the good of his country.

AMBIGUITY.

Ambiguity may be due to the use of words that bear different meanings in different contexts, to the careless use of pronouns, to ellipses, or to the misplacement of words, phrases, or clauses.

EXERCISE XLII.

1. You don't seem to like anything that I do.
2. The scouts reported that they had discovered certain indications of the presence of Indians in the vicinity.
3. I can't find one of my books.
4. I did not promise to accept any offer.
5. He observed that the attendance was smaller than usual.
6. He ate a little pie for dinner.
7. Common sense, Mr. Chairman, is what I want.
8. Did you see the door open? The window broken?
9. You have given me no easy question to answer.
10. The word is not used alone by the uneducated.
11. He said that the mosquitoes would climb up on the trees and bark; that they were very large, and that he had no doubt a great many of them would weigh a pound.
12. Have you heard how old Mrs. J. is?
13. He said he didn't want the cloth any longer.
14. He told his friend that if he did not feel better in half an hour he thought he had better return.
15. Old English poetry was very different from what it is now.

16. When very little snow falls, or when it is blown off the fields, it greatly diminishes the crop of fall wheat the next season.

17. The party of Union and Progress is as superior to the Grits in political morality as they are in patriotism and statesmanship.

18. Men look with an evil eye upon the good that is in others, and think that their reputation obscures them, and that their commendable qualities do stand in their light; and therefore they do what they can to cast a cloud over them, that the bright shining of their virtues may not obscure them.

19. He liked to hear her talk better than any of his associates.

20. He owes a good many more than you.

21. Twelve years ago he came to this town with but one shirt to his back, and now he is worth thousands.

22. The woodshed and contents of Mr. A., O——, was burned last Sunday morning.

23. He wished for nothing more than a dictionary.

24. That is a likeness of the man that painted our house and his wife.

25. Information wanted of J. S., whose mind is a little weak, but otherwise quite harmless.

26. He appeared to have more faith in us than his friends.

27. And thus the son the fervent sire addressed.

28. The Duke yet lives that Henry shall depose.

29. I was not aware that you had been absent till yesterday.

30. He is only quarrelsome when he is drunk.

31. Under the circumstances I must admit that you acted fairly.

32. John Keats, the second of four children, like Chaucer and Spenser, was born in London.

33. Such is the depravity of the world that guilt is more likely to meet with indulgence than misfortune.

34. I came very near losing my way several times.

35. One of our town sportsmen shot 15 brace of partridges, along with a friend, on Saturday last.

36. A few minutes are required after giving the order, to ensure a hot breakfast, which might otherwise seem an unnecessary delay,

37. Whom chance misled his mother to destroy.

38. We import our coffee direct through our agents in New York, which is roasted and ground on the premises daily.

39. The service was impressive, but it lacked either grandeur or beauty.

40. Metal types were now introduced, which before this had been made of wood.

41. Rich or poor you have always been a true friend to me.

42. I thought that the safest plan was to praise everything he did.

43. After some difficulty we reached the gate[,] where we parted from our friend.

44. The next winter[,] which I spent in town happened to be a very mild one.

45. Not a single failure has occurred[,] in consequence of the change in the law.

46. It will be very convenient for those who want access to the original manuscripts.

47. A young man in Ottawa took creosote for the toothache, which nearly poisoned him.

48. I leave my property to my brother and his children in succession.

49. I think you will find my Latin exercise at least as good as his.

50. He was taking a view from a window of the cathedral at Lichfield, in which a party of Royalists had entrenched themselves.

51. It was never intended, as Mr. M. has told you, that the award was not to be adopted unless ratified by the Dominion Parliament.

52. He will scarcely be consoled for the loss which he has sustained by the defeat of the by-law.

53. I said that he was a liar, it is true, and I am sorry for it.

54. The essential elements of a noble manhood are developed only by the personal contact and influence of the true teacher upon the scholar, and this is one of the defects of our system of secondary education.

55. An eye-witness says he saw him bring down a brace of pheasants which rose together unexpectedly in a small cover, each with a single ball from a double-barrelled rifle.

56. Mr. M., 17 West St., has cast off clothing of every description.

57. We will send the brush on trial on receipt of fifty cents, which will be returned if not as represented.

58. The congregation held a very successful bazaar last summer to clear off the debt which remained on the church, and which realized $1500.

59. He continued to execrate the magistrate who committed him without bail in the most profane manner.

60. We wish to express our sincere thanks to our many friends and neighbors for their assistance in the sickness and death of our wife, daughter, and sister.

OBSCURITY.

Obscurity may be due to the use of technical or uncommon terms, to circumlocution or verbosity, to the use of long parentheses, or of long and involved sentences. For obvious reasons it is not worth while to give a formal exercise on this fault. A few illustrations are, however, subjoined. The teacher should point out to his pupils others from their own work.

1. He found on examination a contusion of the integuments under the orbit, with an extravasation of blood and ecchymosis of the surrounding cellular tissue, which was in a tumefied state, and also with a slight abrasion of the cuticle.

2. As man is a microcosm, in whom all the grand principles of the universe converge, making him the essence of their combined action, an epitome of the whole, combining as he does in the elements of his composition those substances that are governed by the same rulings as other organized bodies, differing only in its psychological powers and its ability to answer the telegrams of nature addressed to his senses and conceptions, and contemplate

the great harmonium of the universe with his worthy self as the crown of all its ultimates.

3. The children in our elementary schools are capable of acquiring elementary teaching, without any fear that either their physical or mental energies will be overtasked to an extent which, under the favorable conditions in which our community is happily placed, we can safely venture upon, in comparison with any other community, provided modes of teaching in harmony with nature's laws are required to prevail, and thus aiding and strengthening the child's mental and physical development.

WANT OF FORCE OR HARMONY.

This fault may be due to the use of unnecessary words or of too many connectives, to the presence of many or incongruous statements in the same sentence, to loose sentence-structure or to the awkward repetition of the same (or similarly sounding) words.

EXERCISE XLIII.

1. Hence you will see, therefore, he must necessarily be in error.
2. Several of the spectators who were present voluntarily offered to assist him.
3. He suffered great anxiety of mind in the interval that intervened between his application and their decision.
4. He brought the work to a final completion yesterday.
5. Remember that the period of youth is the time to form correct habits.
6. They will soon have an entire monopoly of the whole trade.
7. That seems to be the universal opinion of all that have seen it working.
8. He went up to him, and awakened him gently, and drew him back from the edge of the precipice, and saved his life.

9. He called his boy, but got no answer, so he searched as far as his chains would permit, but could not find him, so at last he became frantic, and tried to break his chains, but he could not.

10. He asked her to show him her album, which she did, and she called his attention to the likeness of one young lady with whom she had been very intimate when she was attending the Normal School, and who has since attracted attention by her paintings, some of which were exhibited at the Exhibition which was held in T. last fall.

11. When Alexander took Sidon he left his generals to appoint a king, so they went to two brothers and asked one of them to be king, but neither of them would accept, for they said that they were no relation to any former king, and that it would not be right for them to reign, but they told the generals of a man named Abdalonymus, who was related to their former king, but who was so poor that he had to keep a market garden so as to gain a livelihood.

12. I received the books yesterday, and I am very much pleased with them, but you sent me one too many, but I find I may need it, and so I will keep it.

13. He returned to England in 1839, and the next year he was persuaded to enter Parliament, but he soon lost his seat, and then he retired, and pursued his literary tastes, and died suddenly in 1859.

14. It was a practice which he could learn nothing of the origin of.[1]

---

1 "Let me exemplify this tendency away from the native character of the language in the structure of sentences as well as in the choice of words. I refer to the frequent abandonment of that peculiarly characteristic arrangement which puts a preposition at the end of a sentence. This is eminently an English idiom, and nothing but prejudice arising from misapplied analogy with the Southern languages, and the propensity to make style more formal and less idiomatic, could ever have led any one to suppose this construction to be wrong. The false fastidiousness which shuns a short particle at the end of a sentence, is fatal often to a force which belongs to the language with its primal character. The superior-

15. He divided all his property in his lifetime equally among his three sons to avoid any disputes or law suits.

16. He called a meeting of the principal shareholders at his office, secretly, that evening, at the suggestion of the secretary, to consider the matter.

17. He obtained a seat in Parliament, in 1830, through the influence of Lord Lansdowne, where he took an active part.

18. As Clive had all the money he desired; and nothing to occupy his mind, he took opium and died in 1774, being only forty-nine years old.

19. The water-carrier was therefore summoned before the magistrate; but as nothing could be proved against him, he was discharged, but the magistrate kept his donkey.

20. This last year I have spent in preparing for the Institute examination, and have studied Lockwood's Lessons in English and Stopford Brooke's Primer of English Literature.

21. He kept his money in a hole in the floor, where, one rainy night while Silas was away it was found by a man named Dunston Cass, who going past found the cottage empty, walked in, found

---

ity of the idiom I am referring to, could be proved beyond question by examples of the best writing in all the eras of the language. As the error is pretty widespread, let me cite a few of these. Lord Bacon says, 'Houses are built to live in, and not to look on;" and again, 'Revenge is a kind of wild justice, which the more a man's nature runs to, the more ought law to weed it out.' Any attempt to transpose these separable prepositions would destroy the strength and the terseness of the sentences. Even a stronger example occurs in a passage in Donne, one of the great English divines, a contemporary of Bacon's: 'Hath God a name to swear by? . . . Hath God a name to curse by? Hath God a name to blaspheme by? and hath God no name to pray by?' The opening sentence of one of Mr. Burke's most celebrated speeches is—'The times we live in have been distinguished by extraordinary events;' Dr. Franklin's phrase, with its twenty-five Saxon and four Latin words: '. . . William Coleman, then a merchant's clerk about my age, who had the coolest, clearest head, the best heart, and the exactest morals of any man I ever met with.' And observe such a sentence as this of Arnold's, 'Knowledge must be worked for, studied for, thought for; and, more than all, it must be prayed for.' I really think that people, in writing and speaking, might get over their fear of finding a preposition at the end of their sentences."—Reed's *Introduction to English Literature*, quoted in Earle's *English Prose*, pp. 269–70.

the money, and was taking it away when, in the darkness of the night, he fell into a pool and was drowned.

22. That night when he got home he sheltered and kept over night Burley, of Balfour, who helped to murder an archbishop, for which he was caught, and on being taken back his guards stopped over night at the castle of Miles Bellenden.

23. Clive was certainly a very brave and skilful general, and there is but one blot on his character that is not excusable; and that occurred while he was conquering one of the Indian rulers, whose minister he had persuaded to become a traitor, by promising to give the kingdom to him; he swindled the man who was carrying out his scheme, out of his dues by forging the name of a British commander to the agreement and then had another made which did not include the go-between's demands.

24. There also we find a fountain; where, when the Ant has retired to her room and the little maiden awaits her lover, the favorite of the King's court, she sees the princess — who did not accompany her sisters on their flight, but stayed at home, for fear of being caught by her father; who has made her promise him that she would not go out of the castle, without his consent — rise out of the water and speak to her.

25. He exemplified the principal applications of the principle by numerous examples.

26. Each of these forms was formerly divided into two divisions.

27. It is very desirable that all those who desire to compete should be present.

28. It was quite clear to all present that he did not clearly understand the question.

29. He described it in an uninteresting manner.

30. He certainly acted extremely cautiously.

31. I have had occasion to pass the house on several occasions recently.

32. We had never seen or even imagined such a scene.

33. He used many expressions not usually used by good writers.

ERRORS IN THE USE OF FIGURATIVE LANGUAGE.

I. — Inappropriate Metaphors.
II. — Improper Mingling of Metaphors and Literal Statements.
III. — Mixed Metaphors.

EXERCISE XLIV.

1. The *magnum opus* of education is creeping up the steep ascent of efficiency.

2. The questions will naturally partake of the same complexion as his teaching.

3. We must apply the axe to the source of the evil.

4. It should be the prayer of every noble-minded man that the gray dawn of the morning may fade into the brilliant sunlight of noon.

5. The heroic Spanish gunners had no defence but bags of cotton, joined to their own insuperable courage.

6. He flung his powerful frame into the saddle, and his great soul into the cause.

7. The building was surrounded by a mob armed with rustic weapons and ungovernable fury.

8. They were the seven pillars of the new House of Wisdom in the wilderness. In August, 1639, these seven pillars assembled, possessing for the time full power.

9. Our contemporary fancied that he smelled a very large mouse, and in his greediness he was determined to possess it.

10. Now from my fond embrace by tempest torn,
One other column of the state is borne,
Nor took a kind adieu, nor sought consent.

11. No human happiness is so serene as not to contain some alloy.

12. At length Erasmus curbed the wild torrent of a barbarous age.

13. The colonies were not yet ripe to bid adieu to British connection.

14. A torrent of superstition consumed the land.

15. Hope, the balm of life, darts a ray of light into the thick gloom.

16. We must keep the ball rolling, till it becomes a thorn in their sides.

17. There is not a single view of human nature that is not sufficient to extinguish the seeds of human pride.

18. In a moment the thunderbolt was upon them, deluging their country with invaders.

19. I bridle in my struggling muse in vain,
That longs to launch into a bolder strain.

20. On they went, past fertile fields, past vine-clad slopes, halting now and then at young clearings, the abode of the few who had come to lay the corner-stones of future cities on the placid bosom of the broad Ohio.

21. Irregularity of attendance is a log and chain on the progress of instruction, for it blasts and withers the noblest purposes of the best of teachers.

22. There are many considerations which enable me to state that the wave of progress is flowing on to the maturity of perfection.

23. Many embark in the profession without training, experience, or adaptation, and having neither compass nor rudder to guide them, they steer for no particular harbor. This leakage can only be stopped by paying teachers adequate salaries.

24. The knowledge thus acquired, being associated with reason, would not be a passing cloud, and being resident in them it would serve as a pilot to their judgments in solving the problems of life.

25. But although clouds of dusky warriors were seen, from time to time, hovering on the highlands, as if watching their progress, they experienced no interruption.

26. If no authority, not in its nature temporary, were allowed to one human being over another, society would not be employed

in building up propensities with one hand which it has to curb with another.

27. The book contains several other poems however, of a much higher calibre.

28. Presently sinking down into the depths of his own nothingness, he stands absorbed and entranced.

29. The world with all its trials is the furnace through which the soul must pass and be developed before it is ripe for the next world.

30. One of the sources from which has sprung that abundant harvest of usefulness which he has scattered broadcast through the length and breadth of his native land.

31. I was sailing in a vast ocean, without other help than the pole-star of the ancients, and the rules of the French stage.

32. His thoughts soared up from earth like fire, and winged their flight to distant stars.

33. He prayed that the word which had been preached that night might be like a nail driven in a sure place, sending its roots downward and its branches upward, and spreading itself like a green bay-tree.

34. Those whose minds are dull and heavy do not easily penetrate into the folds and intricacies of an affair, and therefore can only scum off what they find at the top.

MISCELLANEOUS ERRORS OF GRAMMAR AND STYLE.

EXERCISE XLV.

1. The reading of the Misses Alice and Mary C., and Master Samuel A., were deserving of special eulogism.

2. The author has kept in mind that clergymen, more than those of any other profession, were likely to study this treatise.

3. Phonetic spelling might obscure the derivation of words, but being that scarcely one out of every hundred persons care about derivation, it would not matter much.

4. Your committee beg to report that they have carefully considered the plans, which we herewith submit for your consideration, and would recommend them for adoption.

5. The desire of wealth, or the desire of equalizing or surpassing others, are neither of them, in themselves either virtuous or vicious.

6. A perfect alphabet of the English language, and of every other language, would contain a number of letters equal to the distinct elementary sounds it contained.

7. Parties having building material laying around cannot be too careful about leaving it close to the road as serious consequences might ensue.

8. He was blamed for pardoning criminals whom public opinion asserted should have expatiated their crimes on the gallows.

9. In this manner we can get news from all parts of the world in a few hours that formerly took days.

10. Bills are requested to be paid quarterly.

11. All hands up that can answer the question.

12. Probably no modern invention, except steam, has done so much for man as the telegraph.

13. Faith in dreams, and in other such superstitions, was carried to a great extent in former times.

14. Miss Lucy D. returned to D. on Saturday, where she is engaged in teaching, on account of the illness of her father.

15. Clive's character was of a persevering nature from boyhood, and with enough troops and money, he could accomplish most anything in India.

16. The amount was subscribed by a few individuals, among whom I find the names of A. and B.

17. Such deviations have not been made without due care and attention being paid to the conflicting opinions of different writers.

18. The writer was further told that if he had anything to say against the book, why did he not come out boldly in print and say it.

19. Most all of the magazines I read including Scribner's, Harper's, Current Literature, Century, and Lippincott's.

20. We would willingly add it to Dr. Hincks' collection of Canadian curiosities, than which we venture to affirm none more curious is at present in the worthy professor's possession.

21. He should be led to understand that he enjoys the scorn and contempt of all honest people.

22. The Board and its officers will be careful to make no entries on the above; or to delay their report after the 20th of January.

23. Nowhere are incredulous blunders to be met with more than in the composition of advertisers.

24. I won't demean myself by striking a gentleman.

25. Canada has arrived at such a state of depression that every day brings new disasters, amounting to the sum of $22,000,000 for the last twelve months.

26. There are no people on the earth, except the Chinese, which have any claim to be called civilized, who are such slaves to local limitations as the French.

27. He undertook to show that the effect of the regulations would be to increase the quality of the pupils, as well as their quantity.

28. Board and lodging is found by chance during the time the character is being formed, without little or any judicious supervision.

29. The wants of our educational system were pressing, and had to be speedily met, as well as defects removed, and improvements supplied.

30. There is also many questions taken to him by the children in Arithmetic which he fails to tell them how to do, and cannot do them himself.

31. He was well calculated by his vigor and activity to cope with the wild country to be surveyed and its still wilder inhabitants.

32. The opportunity was presented of adjusting the functions of these institutions so that the work of each should find its proper point of contact, and not overlap each other.

33. I have been told that people will not buy sewing machines, except from peddlers who will talk them into buying the kind they are selling and running down all others.

34. Any person who wants to get either of these articles, by writing me, and saying the kind of sewing machine or organ they want, and if I cannot get it for them at the wholesale price I will let them know.

35. Two substantives, when they come together and do not signify the same thing, the former must be in the possessive.

36. The fact is patent that without due examination, or useless because ineffective examination, the book has been sanctioned.

37. The verb is a word that states what a thing does or is done to.

38. At the same time Clarkson, Wilberforce, Fox, and Pitt were endeavoring to abolish that relic of barbarism, the African slave-trade, which, after twenty years of persistent effort, both in Parliament and out, they at last accomplished.

39. The several hospitals are open to the students under the guidance of a corps of able professors and practitioners who will take ample pains to illustrate the same at the bedside.

40. In case where a large amount of ashes are to be removed on the regular day for the district, special arrangements must be made at the office of the Street Department, City Hall, at least twenty-four hours before the same are to be removed.

41. He searches with avidity for the hidden causes, and with his skilful hand makes loose their bonds, and frees the sufferer from its ruthful folds.

42. The vain pretender has sunk in the whirlpool of his own ruin, carrying with him the innocent and unwary, with saddened hearts to surviving friends, who are made the sad victims of their own confidence.

43. What would you think of the safety of an ocean steamer, freighted with human life, looking onward with palpitating hearts to meet dear ones in a far-off land, whose engine was run by a person who could not name the parts of his machinery, or knew its capacity or the limits of its power?

44. Feeling the necessity for a more thorough system of medical training, and a more familiar acquaintance with the medical sciences and their collateral branches than is required in the prescribed course of medical studies, and the time in which to become conversant with the branches taught, as are laid down in their course by the majority of medical colleges in our country, it was deemed expedient to establish a school, etc.

45. The Kings of Denmark and Norway invaded England, and spreading themselves over the country committed many depredations.

46. In a few days I will more fully explain to you my views and claims on your suffrages, which I consider equal to any candidate which might offer himself for your approbation.

47. In both cases a customer can sit as long as he pleases; but those of the first class have also the right of taking their cups to the third story and smoke as well as read while enjoying his drink whatever it may be.

48. Last Sunday a new programme was entered upon, printed at this office, which we think will add to the interest in its exercises.

49. After that I shall begin to think that nothing is too strange to be incredible.

50. In England we are said to learn manners at second hand from your side of the water, and that we dress our behavior in the frippery of France.

51. Mr. A. Please accept my best thanks for the very prompt and liberal settlement of my fire loss of $10.75 in full from the above company which occurred on Friday, 16th inst., four days after the occurrence to my full and entire satisfaction.

52. I will still continue to sell for cash, and no second price, thereby enabling me to offer my customers unusual good value.

53. Trusting by strict application to business, and determined to second my position by offering the best value in this country, I trust not only to retain my present large connection but a larger increase for the future.

54. They approved of the recommendation for the retirement of the Principal from his office, whom they found was desirous of retiring by reason of impaired health.

55. We are not an offensive society, but on the contrary slow to take offence and offer none, act as Christians, and no intoxicating liquor was allowed in our lodges.

56. The cultivation of the soil, the most honorable and independent industry with which men or women could be engaged, being abandoned by those best able to make it pay, impoverishes the country.

57. Not finding the cash box, which was the object of his visit, he took the key of the store from Mr. M's pocket, and repaired thither, which place he ransacked pretty well.

58. He hoped the members of the order would make a note of the fact that our present Prime Minister, who had lately visited the R. C. Cathedral in Quebec, and took part in the celebration of high mass, was one of the most shameful pieces of hypocrisy that was ever perpetrated.

59. He begs to draw their attention to the fact that owing to having almost the exclusive sale of books used in the Collegiate Institute enables him to buy largely, and thereby able to give the best discount.

60. We, the undersigned electors of the ward of St. G., having viewed the government of our civic affairs for the past twelve months, the recent exposure of public documents and the failure of securing pure and good water, as well as general improvements in the ward, demand an immediate change, and therefore having a knowledge of your business qualifications and integrity, respectfully request, etc.

61. We the undersigned electors of St. L. ward, knowing that you have been prominently connected with the interests of the east end for many years, and being also a large ratepayer, together with many other qualifications, we deem you admirably fitted to represent our interests at the Council Board, and therefore request, etc.

62. Gentlemen,—Although my real estate interests in your ward being equal to many of you, I feel I would be wanting in duty if I did not appreciate the motive you had in view, and I cannot find language to express my gratitude for the intended honor to be conferred on me.

63. A truly national system of education is as much concerned in rearing up a moral and intelligent population, and securing honesty and fair dealing as essential qualities of every citizen, as well as mental culture.

64. The Committee are of opinion that the papers for the Intermediate should be different from those for the Teachers' Examination, and so to preserve to the former its true object, of being a test for such moderate proficiency as pupils generally after the course of two years in the High School might reasonably be expected to attain, in order to pass from the lower to the upper school, and the Intermediate to cease to be a barrier between the lower and upper school.

65. The college has always possessed a distinctive element in nearly one-half of its pupils being resident, and so subjected when under wholesome influences to a further process of intellectual development, and which in the experience of other countries, as well as the fiftieth year of the college itself, has been found advantageous.

66. The number of day pupils, especially in the lower forms, interfere with a larger element of resident boarders, as well as the inferior boarding house accommodation; and the high rates paid by boarders, both for tuition fees and board dues, and which, as one of the objects of the Provincial endowment, should be rendered more accessible to the parents of the pupils throughout the

Province, who may desire to avail themselves of the special advantages afforded by the discipline and other educational influences, of the College residence.

67. The letter brought a deputation of three persons on board. The lieutenant informed them verbally that he had orders to set fire to all seaport towns between Boston and Halifax.

68. We shall be satisfied if we can throw any additional light upon a subject of such vital importance to those who are its unfortunate victims.

69. The beneficial effects of Cod Liver Oil in Consumption has become a proverb.

70. In September, 1877, my health began to fail and my physician pronounced it spinal trouble.

71. The price is one dollar per bottle, or six bottles for five dollars, and can be obtained from druggists and dealers in medicine generally throughout the United States.

72. These facts being apparent to the medical profession, and knowing, as they do, its intrinsic virtues, we have been induced by them to prepare it in an emulsion.

73. Soon after the patient commences its use the appetite and digestion are improved, and a demand is created for food that has not existed before.

74. We will guarantee from its use better results in the various diseases for which it is adapted than any single or combined remedy in existence.

75. On account of its nauseous properties and the difficulty of administering it, especially to children, where it is most useful, it has come largely into disuse and been substituted by pills and purgatives.

76. Common sense teaches if it is instrumental in curing the racking cough of the consumptive that has lasted for months, why should it not cure a cough of a few weeks' duration.

77. Reason teaches us to suggest that if the patient is sensibly affected by cold, the mild and equitable climate of the South would seem to be advisable.

78. It must be borne in mind, however, that although a remedy may possess wonderful curative properties its usefulness is greatly impaired unless perfect obedience to the laws of health are conformed to.

79. We believe we are warranted in making the statement that more physicians in this country prescribe it than any other remedy known in the Materia Medica except it may be quinine.

80. We must confess to a sense of satisfaction in producing a remedy that has the entire sanction of the medical profession, as well as being almost a specific for this dreadful scourge.

81. We sincerely hope you will read carefully these pages, and if you have been fortunate enough to escape from this relentless foe, be kind enough to send it to some friend who requires the medical and life-giving properties that it presents.

82. A resolution was adopted pledging those present to murder the jurymen who convicted Louise Michel at the first opportunity.

83. Some of the younger pupils seemed to enjoy it, but to the older ones the lecture was not so appreciative as expected.

84. The above reward will be paid for information that will lead to the arrest and conviction of the person or persons who set fire to either the barns of D. E. or of G. H. S., which have been lately destroyed.

85. Regulations. (3) A professional gardener will decide on the merits of the plants, by whom any violation of the preceding regulations will be detected, and such exhibitors will be excluded from any share in the prizes awarded.

86. Wanted, a saddle horse for a young lady, gentle and well trained. Apply at No. —, E St.

87. Several candidates who might otherwise have earned high marks are reduced by gross errors in Orthography.

88. Parents have to suffer loss for the depredations of their children when at home, and why not abroad?

89. For several hours no sound save the calls of the pheasants were heard in the forest.

90. An advertisement appeared in Saturday's *Mail* to the effect that there was a good opening in M. for a doctor, having no name or address attached.

91. A few friends of the deceased followed the remains to Evergreen Cemetery, where they were quietly interred in a new lot, without services or ceremony.

92. Among the many anxious eyes that saw for the first time the blue, hazy hills of the new land wherein they were to try their fortunes, was a small family group, one of which was a bright-eyed little boy of five years old

93. I have been much pleased with the excellent papers which have appeared in the *Journal* during the past year, and for this I am sure the educational staff of Ontario as a whole are grateful.

94. This is to certify that I attended Mrs. M. in her last illness, which was caused by a fall upon the ice, and that she died in consequence thereof.

95. In no case should the body be exposed to view: no public funeral held, and as few attend as possible.

96. As the stag fights at bay, with a heroism such as despair alone begets, so fought the Pole and his followers under the hail of bullets which sang around them.

97. During the forenoon the American gunboat *Michigan* began to patrol the river to prevent any breaches of the neutrality laws; and shut her eyes whenever a boat with reinforcements or stores for O'Neill happened to be crossing from the American shore.

98. I would advocate the establishment of schools where children of mothers who are obliged to work the whole day to gain a livelihood for their children, and who are in the meantime abandoned on the streets, would be cared for and get their dinners and be returned to their homes in the evening, or some of the children might bring their dinners.

99. The postmaster has received a communication from a sailor near O., informing him of the death of a man named J. S., who once lived near here, by falling off their boat in a gale and getting drowned, and wished his friends to know.

100. We are told to look at the county of X., who so nobly provided a house of refuge for their poor, and it only costs that county one dollar and eighty-three cents per week for each inmate.

101. We have been led to make a closer examination of the books to see if they be what some rival firms have declared them to be, or if they be what their publisher asserts.

102. The king had charged him, therefore, to provide fit lodging and entertainment for him until he had time to see him.

103. An urgent appeal was made to all friends of the University to boldly make demand to the State to more liberally support the Provincial College.

104. Mutual Marriage Aid Association. The following benefits have been paid during the last year, any of which will give information by enclosing stamp.

105. While oiling the gearing of the machine his hand got caught in it, nearly taking it off.

106. I am very much pleased that the committee in some degree have attended to my request, in revising some of the errors in their late manifesto, however much more so had the errors not occurred.

107. This is an important error, quite sufficient to deter or otherwise hinder intending immigrants towards this country.

108. I trust the committee will continue revising other errors and that these corrections may have as wide or wider circulation than the report.

109. The exceptions to the report were broad rather than specific, believing, as the errors were so absurd, that the committee should discover as well as correct their errors.

110. The worthy objects of this entertainment will no doubt receive the encouragement it deserves on the part of the citizens of Toronto.

111. They proceeded to the inner court of the palace, where their comrades were already drawn up and under arms — the squires each standing behind their masters.

112. He said that in his forty years' observance of the liquor traffic he saw not a single redeeming feature of the traffic.

113. There are a number of names likely to be brought before the convention, any one of whom would make a good representative.

114. It enters its twenty-fifth volume with more voluntary *bona fide* readers, and more legitimate advertisers than few Canadian country journals can boast of.

115. The entertainment netted the scholars in the neighborhood of $60, which will be immediately invested in the purchase of gymnasium appliances, and will form an appurtenance to the High School.

116. There has been an unusual number of bank failures in the U. S. during the past week, and of these at least two are distinctly traceable to the speculating propensities of its cashier or other prominent officer.

117. Any person giving information as will lead to its recovery will be paid for his trouble and thankfully received.

118. Some years intervened before his next speech and nearly every one of the veterans of '76 were dead when Webster again ascended the platform with the solid shaft of granite behind it.

119. To talk to a man in a state of moral corruption to elevate himself by contemplating the abstract conception of holiness, is somewhat a similar absurdity as to ask a blind man to admire the beauty of color.

120. When we say this we mean that the Romans put the ideas which we express by these three verbs into a different shape to that which we employ; and that in neither of the three they made use of a transitive verb combined with its nearest object.

121. Ideas rejected peremptorily at the time often rankle, and bear fruit by and by.

122. Thus by the dispensations of Providence the control, as well as the support which a father exercises over his family, were suddenly withdrawn.

123. Whereas untrue representations of the whole colonization

work have been industriously circulated to serve personal and political ends, which statements though not directed against any particular company, nevertheless justice and decency compel us to give them a flat denial so far as this company is concerned.

124. There was no pledged majority to remove him, but as it was supposed that he would resign at the next meeting, and finding that he had no intention of doing so, a feeling existed that his resignation was being withheld for political purposes.

125. The heroism of the females of the Revolution has passed from memory with the generation that witnessed it.

126. He don't venture to complain of the material information that Colonel Harley kept from him.

127. Too many innovations should not be attempted at once, unless where there happens to be, as in Chemistry, a predisposition to admit them.

128. The present low freights have increased business to some extent. The supply of produce, however, being small, has materially checked the number of shipments.

129. They would have sent him to his account with as little compunction as Jael sent the Canaanite captain, or they would have blessed the arm that did it with as much eloquence as Deborah.

130. The Mayor is anxious to cover up his tracks, but they are too transparent to be swallowed by an intelligent people without a grimace.

131. Mr. M. having become convinced that certain correspondence emanating from B., and which he unmercifully berated a respectable citizen, Mr. H., for writing, has tendered him an ample apology.

132. I have only to say to the electors that I run for the office upon the recommendation and support of many influential citizens, amounting to me to as much as is claimed by the so-called regularly nominated candidate.

133. He called upon them to stamp it out with an iron hand, and to see to it that none of the guilty parties would escape.

134. These goods are of exceptionally good value notwithstanding the extraordinary low prices at which they are offered. In corsets we guarantee satisfaction, and will refund the money paid if not worn longer than three weeks.

135. The vessel made for the shore, and when the boats were lowered all crowded into them, and reached the beach in safety, where the settlers received them with the greatest kindness, and shelter and food were provided for them till the arrival of the steamer.

136. La Jeunesse brought coffee, such as we only taste on the continent.

137. It was not my intention to stand as a candidate, but being requested by such an influential and dignified catalogue of names, all of whom are as deeply interested in the welfare of the Township as I am, I will accede to your very amiable request, hoping the position you desire me to fulfil may merit the kind approbation and hearty concurrence of the general ratepayers of the Township.

138. At the close of the year the farmer, instead of being harassed and put out at the never-failing yellow envelope containing an account far exceeding his expectations, for your accounts are always larger than you expect if you go on tick, or else he receives a notice requesting prompt attention to a note shortly coming due, compelling him to hitch up, fetch a load of grain to market, and take what he can get for it; what a difference, I say, if he and his wife had managed to pay as they went.

139. He blames Nuncomar's death on Impey whom he thinks did not act right.

140. I will pay the above reward to any one who will prove that the above facts are untrue.

141. He has now the management of the institution, and his success or otherwise will show who among them we are to consider responsible for its past record.

142. He bounded over the fence, which his pursuers essaying to do failed, and came to grief very badly.

143. Having had the misfortune to injure his thumb in the third innings, through his incapacity they lost the game.

144. We will guarantee to do for you fully equal, if not a little better, than any establishment in our surroundings.

145. Every exercise must be certified as being the candidate's own work, and should show his progress during at least three months.

146. His frailties, which none of us are without, were of the head, not of the heart.

147. We have nothing to say against written examinations sparingly and judicially used.

148. No person will deny but what there are acts done by such persons which would be better if left undone.

149. The price of the book is $4, free by mail, which should accompany the order.

150. This balsam will, and has saved the life of thousands attacked by croup, where it has been taken in season.

151. Before the officers could reach the house the bird and his brave wife had flown and escaped capture.

152. As we purpose attending personally to our business, and having a thorough practical knowledge of the trade, any person favoring us with their patronage can rest assured of making thoroughly good bargains.

153. You have great cause to be thankful for the many temptations from which you have been saved.

154. Hastings, although he did not do the work yet he supplied the means, and in this way he was responsible for the cruel war, and for which he afterwards lost his office.

155. The anticipation of this gain rests on two assumptions which are tacitly taken for granted, but both of them erroneous.

156. The boy brought it to him and he sent it to Bob Cratchit's, his nephew, who he disliked for marrying a person who he thought he shouldn't have.

157. Parties who anticipate purchasing an organ or piano would save money by calling or corresponding with me.

158. They were planned by a clever servant, who, to say all that can be said in his praise, is that he is worthy of such a master.

159. We do not believe that this is so universal a fault as the other; yet teachers tell pupils too many things that they could dig out for themselves, and thus gain strength for new conquests.

160. I should have written you sooner, but neglected it, but hope I am not too late yet, so hoping I will receive it by your kindness, and you will much oblige yours truly.

161. Monday, the 13th July, was duly celebrated by the Orangemen of the district, it being the 190th anniversary of the battle of the Boyne, in a manner of no discredit to the organization.

162. About 11 A.M. they had the misfortune of being the recipients of a most drenching shower, which had the tendency to put a damper for a time to their enjoyment.

163. To try to give a synopsis of both the sermons, which were both eloquent and able, would not give justice to him and must be heard to be appreciated.

164. A man nowadays is confronted with the very serious question, how to make a living, and unless he is an unusually bright specimen the most of his time is taken up in searching for a satisfactory answer.

165. The pastor occupied the chair in his usual happy style, and opened the meeting by prayer, and after a few words congratulatory to those present, and the great pleasure he felt from the general appearance all around him, felt thankful to the Head of the Church for the harmony and unity which still prevails.

166. Here Evangeline decided to remain the winter, because Gabriel had said that he would return there in the spring.

167. Fitz-James wounded Roderick three times, who soon felt the loss of blood and began to shower blows fiercer than ever; but his rage was no match for the Saxon's skill, who soon forced Roderick's sword from him and brought him to his knees.

168. Never date a check ahead or draw for more than you have in the bank, even though the person you give it to promises

to keep it until a given date. Nine times out of ten they won't do it.

169. After their entrance to the village the procession was formed on the market square, the routine being followed, and marched through the different thoroughfares which were handsomely decorated with arches, and the usual mottoes appeared on them.

170. The English wanted to impose a duty and the Americans would not pay it, so the English thought they would make them, so they raised an army and went over to America, but the Americans would not be beaten, and so after a great many battles the Americans gained their independence.

171. The Rohilla war was caused by Surajah Dowlah wanting to get possession of their country, and he had no claim to it, and they thought just as much of their country as he did of his, and they were not a people to be fooled with, for they were no cowards and were very brave and skilful in war.

172. He stayed two years longer at school and was looking forward to going to college when his uncle died and left him to the care of a friend, named C., who was anxious to rid himself of the charge, so he obtained a writership in the East India Company whither he proceeded after spending a few months at a commercial academy to study arithmetic.

173. There were two other boats, but too small to hold the whole number, and an attempt was made to make a raft, but the beating of the waves made this impossible, so that the men already in the pinnace were directed to lie down in the bottom, and pack themselves like herrings in a barrel, while the lesser boats returned through the surf to pick off the rest, a most difficult matter — and indeed some had to be dragged off on ropes, and others to swim, but not one was lost.

174. The boats picked up as many as was possible, without overloading them, and then made for the shore, which was only two miles off, hoping to land these and return for more, but the surf ran so high that landing was impossible, and after seeking till

daylight for a safe landing place they were at last picked up by a schooner, which then made for the wreck, where thirty or forty were still clinging to the masts in a dreadful state of exhaustion.

175. The ships of the enemy having been seen first from these, the signal was given to Hasdrubal, and the excitement began on land and in the camp sooner than at the sea coast and the ships, the sound of the oars and the other noise of the sailors having not yet been heard, and the headlands concealing the fleet, when suddenly one horseman after another sent by Hasdrubal orders those wandering on the shore and those quiet in the tents, expecting nothing less that day than the enemy or a battle, to go on board the ships hastily and to take up arms; that the Roman fleet was now not far from the harbor. — *Livy*, xxii. 19.[1]

176. These things having been learned, thc chiefs of Britain who, after the battle had taken place, had come together to do those things which Cæsar had ordered, having conferred among

[1] "In the classical schools, teachers of Greek and Latin may do much to help the cause of good English without going out of their way. They may insist, for example, that every translated sentence, whether spoken or written, shall be a good English sentence at all points. This is done in England; and hence it is that Eton and Harrow boys, though they receive little training in their own language by itself, write better English than American boys of the same age. This is done in France; and hence it is that every educated Frenchman writes idiomatic French.

"In this country too, I am happy to say, attention is beginning to be paid to English by teachers of other subjects. In several quarters, students in Latin or Greek, French or German, are encouraged to make a translation a means of enriching their English vocabulary, and enlarging their knowledge of English idioms. The master of one academy within my knowledge does not allow his pupils to make the ordinary word-for-word translation of the Latin ablative absolute. He insists that the sentence 'Tarquin having been expelled, two consuls began to be created instead of one king,' or the sentence, 'No one will be about to be a thief, we being the aid,' is not an English sentence, is not the English equivalent of the Latin. At least one college has, at the instance of the English instructor, inserted the following words in its statement of the requirements for admission to the Freshman Class: 'The passages set for translation must be rendered into simple and idiomatic English. Teachers are requested to insist on the use of good English as an essential part of the candidate's training in translation' — a requirement which if strictly enforced, cannot fail to tell for good upon the candidate's command of his mother-tongue." — Hill, *Our English*, p. 24.

themselves, when they understood that cavalry and ships and corn were wanting to the Romans, and learned the fewness of the soldiers from the smallness of the camp, which was even smaller on this account, because Cæsar had brought over the legions without baggage, thought the best thing to be done was, a rebellion having been made, to cut off our men from corn and supplies, and to prolong the thing into the winter, because, these having been conquered or cut off from a return, they trusted that no one would afterwards pass over to Britain for the purpose of making war.— *Cæsar*, B. G., iv. 30.

177. Cicero, who through all the previous days had kept his soldiers in the camp by the orders of Cæsar with the greatest diligence, and had not even suffered a servant to go beyond the fortification, on the seventh day, distrusting from the number of days that Cæsar would keep his word, because he heard that he had advanced farther, nor was any report brought of his return; at the same time influenced by the talk of those who called his forbearance almost a siege, if indeed it were not permitted them to go out of the camp, and expecting no event of such a kind by which harm could be done within three miles of the camp, nine legions and a very large body of cavalry being opposed to the enemy, and the enemy being dispersed and almost destroyed, sent five cohorts to the nearest cornfields to gather corn, between which and the camp there was in all one hill.— *Cæsar*, B. G., vi. 36.

178. Cæsar, after his exhortation to the tenth legion, having set out to the right wing, when he saw that his men were hard pressed, and the standards of the twelfth legion having been brought into one place, that the soldiers being crowded together were themselves a hindrance to themselves for fighting; all the centurions of the fourth cohort having been slain, and the standard-bearer having been killed, the standard having been lost, almost all the centurions of the rest of the cohorts having been wounded or killed, among these the chief centurion, Baculus, a most brave man, having been exhausted by many and severe wounds, so that he could not sustain himself; that the rest were more tardy and that

some in the rear being deserted by their leaders were withdrawing from the battle and avoiding the weapons; that the enemy did not cease coming up in front from the lower ground, and were pressing on on each flank, and that things were in a desperate state, nor was there any reinforcement which could be sent; having snatched a shield from a soldier in the rear (for he himself had come there without a shield), advanced to the front rank, and having called the centurions by name, and having exhorted the rest of the soldiers, ordered them to advance and to open out the maniples, in order that they might be able to use their swords more easily.— *Cæsar*, B. G., ii. 25.

Part V.

TYPICAL EXAMINATION PAPERS.

HARVARD UNIVERSITY.

Specimens of Bad English.

I.

1. The vote of the trustees on the resolution sustaining President Bartlett, was six in the affirmative, four in the negative, with one member of the board absent, whom it is claimed by the opposition would have voted in the negative.

2. "I only said I wouldn't go, without one of the servants come up to Sir Leicester Dedlock," returns Mr. Smallweed.

3. Neither Senators Dawes nor Hoar were in their seats to-day.

4. She was smaller in stature than either of her three sisters, to all of whom had been acceded the praise of being fine women.

5. Happily neither she nor her mother had completely parted with their senses.

6. "If I review Virgil for instance in April, I will forget much of it before July, having so much other work on my hands."

7. "Lying off the Battery, we would be as easily accessible as are vessels at the city piers."

"When will you be ready for business?" asked the reporter.

"By the spring of 1883; but not before. . . . We shall have a stock company, but there will be comparatively little stock issued. We shall place a large amount of bonds. This will enable us to avoid onerous taxation from the city"

8. He folded it and put it in his breast pocket and laid down once more, and it was not referred to again.

9. Although Mr. Jonas conducted Charity to the hotel and sat himself beside her at the board, it was pretty clear that he had an eye to "the other one" also, for he often glanced across at Mercy, and seemed to draw comparisons between the personal appearance of the two, which were not unfavorable to the superior plumpness of the younger sister.

10. "This is a phenomena common to an immense number of diseases."

11. "Mr. Stanley was the only one of his predecessors who slaughtered the natives of the region he passed through."

12. "She was a good deal hurt, and her hand so severely injured that unless she has the forefinger amputated, she will entirely lose the use of it."

13. "The farmstead was always the wooden, white painted house of which all the small country towns are composed."

14. If I were old enough to be married, I am old enough to manage my husband's house.

15. The seventeenth century evidently had a different notion of books and women than that which flourishes in the nineteenth.

16. "It would not suit the rules of art nor of my own feelings to write in that style."

Entrance Examination, June, 1882.

II.

1. "He is a man of the lowest principles, and by his intrigues he makes an easy dupe of most every one."

2. "Iago was Othello's ancient and in whom he placed the greatest confidence."

3. "By his cunningness he enticed people to believe him "honest," which we will soon see was not so. He was fearless to tell a lie."

4. "Then he inaugurates a quarrel with him, which soon spreads over the whole camp."

5. "After seeking to ackomplish his purpose by informing Othello of different acts of intimacy, and had caused him to be on the alert, he told him that he had seen the handkerchief in Cassios' hands. In this state of mind it required very little evidence to thoroughly convince him of his guilt."

6. "He had that insight into human character which enabled him to know how to approach every one and take advantage of their weak points."

7. "Few of Shakspere's characters but what have their regretful moments, few are lost to better feelings yet in the character of Iago one must search deeply to find a moral quality."

8. "These two poets in the hands of such actors; as Booth and Salvini, make the play one of the most pleasing, that is played in our time."

9. "He is none of your great blustering fellows who goes around knocking people on the head, but in appearance a gentleman, Othello's lieutenant."

10. "When his money was at an end, these unprincipled friends began to look cold upon him."

11. "The countless number of mathematical propositions is suspended for a few axioms."

12. "If the present generation have erred, its errors have been due to humanity, and Christian hopefulness of good."

Entrance Examination, September, 1882.

III.

1. I do'nt see anything so very particular in having a few almanacks; other people have them, I believe, as well as me.

2. Neither Emily or Valancourt were conscious how they reached the chateau.

3. We should not punish a breach of the Sabbath, nor any offence against the Mosaic law.

4. In intellectual and moral strength Maggie Tulliver is what George Eliot was; in physical beauty she is what George Eliot would have chosen to have been.

5. Mr. Freeman may not know but little more history than he would if Macaulay had never written.

(*From papers written by candidates for admission to Harvard College.*)

6. But when he learned that Orlando was the son of the deposed Duke's friend, his brow clouded, and he bade Orlando to immediately leave the city, or his life would be in danger.

7. His forbearance toward everyone even his enemies strikes us at once as we read of his forbearance toward Pope although he might easily have found weapons far better than those of Pope and which he certainly could have used with as much skill.

8. The son of the old noble, being treated illy by his oldest brother, goes to the court of the userping duke. There he wrestles with the pugilist and overcomes him, which feat in connection with his good looks has a very bad effect upon Rosalind the daughter of the true duke, in other words she falls in love with him.

9. But when the King asked him: "who was his father" and learning him to be the sun of Sir Rowland de Bois his countenance changed and he said: I would you were any other man's son, than Sir Rowland, for he was an enemy to me and so you must be.

10. Celia weds Oliver, the brother of Orlando, who has again kindly received the latter to his home. The deep and true affection of Orlando and Rosalind, the ridiculous sayings of Touchstone, and the artless Audrey, are all pleasing factors which go to make up the tale.

11. Orlando tells Rosalind, whom he thinks is a shepherd boy, how he is in love with a lady who had once rewarded him at a wrestling match, and that if he could only find her he would offer himself to her.

12. After several days had transpired Rosalind told Orlando that she would, on a certain day cause Rosalind to be present when he could have her as his wife.

13. At last the appointed day arrived, and from far and near people flocked to see the sport, among whom being Celia, Frederick's daughter, and Rosalind, her cousin, daughter of the banished duke.

14. The day for the match came, and when, shortly before the eventful time, Orlando walked onto the field, his face and youthful look attracted the attention of Duke Frederick, and Rosalind and Celia.

15. Everybody except his brother, tried to persuade him from his made intention, but he would not hear them.

16. Orlando was urged on, by his brother, to the match who wished to destroy him, and who, failing in this, at last caused him to flee to the forest.

17. Hospitality was one of Addison's characteristics, and he rarely met a friend, but what he asked him to his lodgings to have a talk over a bottle of wine.

18. In parliament, Addison never spoke but once.

September, 1883.

IV.

1. The wealth of the many make a very little show in statistics; the wealth of the few make a great show in statistics.

2. By "Good Use is meant the correct use of correct words in their correct, places, no more than necessary, and to always use the simplest words.

3. I think the style bad and that he has a good deal of the old woman in his way of thinking.

4. If you were able to go to church tomorrow, you will hear an excellent sermon.

5. One sailor said: "I never saw anything to equal it, and as long as I live I will never be able to forget those terrible and pitiful cries for help."

6. The Commission in their report also speaks of S's Copyright.

7. In their compartment of the train going back to Paris who should they see but Mr. Stuyvesant, who had been to Versailles, not as a pleasure trip, but on a matter of business.

8. Then we honor most of all, perhaps, he whose anniversary comes this month, the great Luther.

9. If the person who took a black silk umbrella out of Sever 32 by mistake, he would much oblige the owner by returning the same to ——.

10. It keeps in good repair, does the writing well, and is a real pleasure to operate it.

11. There are points where in my mind Wordsworth reaches as high if not higher, than any poet of his time.

12. It happens, therefore, that there are active and influential members of such conventions whom their fellow-delegates, who know them at all, know perfectly well ought to be "in durance vile."

13. Charles was the first to die, although out of his slender gains he had put by as much as would have provided comfortably for Mary after his death.

14. He is endorsed by the citizens of Springfield, Mass., and also by Major General Howard, which document he will be happy to show at any time.

15. President McCosh and Eliot each of whom was a member of the University crew of their respective colleges excelled in athletics.

16. In fact, there is no case of disease among Horses and Cattle where these valuable Powders are not called for, and by their timely administration will save the lives of many valuable animals.

17. Everything Scott described he has made famous and none can go to the Highlands but what they must visit the places he describes.

18. In these days it does not seem hardly possible that any man with such an education and poetic genius as Coleridge himself possessed would have expressed such an opinion.

19. An arrangement which sandwiches a sermon or a biblical lecture between each chapter of the story—a great convenience for skippers.

20. Accordingly as a man combines these characteristics, will he be an admirer of Scott and Dickens.

June, 1884.

V.

1. Pitt and Fox both died a month after each other.

2. His mother was a tight-rope dancer who lost her life while performing that feat.

3. Charles died a promising young clergyman, to the intense grief of his family and a large circle of friends.

4. The patent "Austria" skate fastens itself by stepping into it.

5. Here we were obliged to wait for day-break in order to make a landing, which, being made in a small boat, was rendered very difficult on account of the swiftness of the current.

6. After a hearty breakfast we left the camp, at which we had arrived the night before, about half-past seven on a cool September morning, in an old fashioned farm wagon, for we had some distance to go, and the walking through the tall brown-grass of the prairie is fatiguing in the extreme.

7. Mr. Smith presents his Compliments to Mr. Jones, and finds he has a Cap which isn't mine. So if you have a Cap which isn't his, no doubt they are the Ones.

8. My Christian and surname begin and end with the same letters.

9. Charlemagne patronized not only learned men, but also established educational institutions.

10. Because there are a few savage tribes who have no beliefs whatsoever, is no more, on the contrary not as great, a cause than to say, there is or are divine beings.

11. The crows whirled over his head, at which he now and then shied a stone.

12. They found grandmamma and luncheon there, with open arms and inviting dishes to welcome them.

13. I had heard of him [Keats] as an original, but peculiar, genius, the rich budding of whose thoughts was destined never to be perfected by an untimely death.

14. Quite a number of Harvard's most noted professors were present at Prof. Thompson's lecture, President Eliot being among the number.

15. Mrs. Jones, who is now 84, gave her first ball more than 60 years ago, at her house in Bowling Green, which shows the rapid growth of the city.

16. Nonquit does not possess a store of any kind; not even a barber shop. The ladies miss the former; the latter is an inconvenience to the gentlemen.

17. Mme. Adelina Patti having consented to appear as Martha, and Mme. Scalchi as Nancy, that favorite opera will be performed on Tuesday evening next.

18. The Amherst college senate has overhauled the '86 Olio, it being claimed that articles were published in that production which had been especially forbidden by the faculty.

19. When moulting we should take great care of canary birds.

20. These tickets will be good from Saturday A. M. until Sunday night, and by paying a small sum in adition, will be good from Friday afternoon to Monday night, so that those who wish to accompany the nine on the whole trip can use the same tickets.

June, 1885.

VI.

1. These chapters prove that the boy Grant and the man Grant were as nearly alike as bud and flower — that the latter cannot be accounted for without the former is studied.

2. It is a pity these things are not more studied by the elaborate, and that in addition to reading Mr. Gladstone's and Mr.

Chamberlain's speeches, they would sometimes read also Lord Granville's despatches.

3. This is one of the reasons why the author did, and every one else ought to love nature.

4. A convent, a lunatic asylum, or a husband—either will do.

5. Colonel Enderby stepped out onto the gravel.

6. If I was you, I wouldn't let my husband talk in that way.

7. One alumnae recently pledged $5000 for improvements in the opportunities for physical culture at Vassar, on condition that $5000 should be raised by the alumnae.

8. A celebrated anatomist, a profound chemist, and one of the first physiologists in Europe, it was a relief to him to turn from these subjects.

9. In proportion as either of these two qualities are wanting, the language is imperfect.

10. Madame Voss had a clearer insight to the state of her niece's mind than had her husband.

11. A British and a Yankee skipper were sailing side by side.

12. She had not spoken hardly above a word during that interview.

13. We may fairly regard the book as a collection of youthful reflections as to the advisibility of publishing which the poet had not yet made up his mind and perhaps had he lived would have suppressed.

14. He considered it his duty to remonstrate with a woman whom he plainly saw was very much out of place there.

15. On reaching the office he heard a door creak in the basement, and upon going down stairs some one ran up.

16. The roof covers quite a considerable amount of ground.

17. Lord D——, whose good nature was unbounded and which, in regard to myself, had been measured by his compassion perhaps for my condition, faltered at this request.

18. I never heard him say he had, and I would be likely to know.

19. These figures are certainly conclusive as to the ability of

veterans to more than hold their own under existing circumstances.

20. The Yale News complains of smoking in their gymnasium.

June, 1886.

VII.

1. Being commissioned to relieve the beleagured city, she sat out at the head of a force whose numbers were swelled by accessions all along the march.

2. It is not too much to say that he is known most and best by a single story; one which we read in childhood and seem never to quite forget.

3. It is most efficacious when taken fasting and mixed with an equal quantity of hot water.

4. De la Marck, in short, saw he would not be supported, even by his own band, in any farther act of immediate violence.

5. Tom stared at me, and I wished I was home.

6. Mr. Hastings did not reveal this to Mr. Marley, who, by the way, had fallen in love with Miss Hardcastle, whom he thought was the bar-maid.

7. When every worldly maxim arrayed itself against him; when blasted in fortune, and disgrace and danger darkened around his name, she loved him the more ardently for his very sufferings.

8. In seeing Miss Anderson's Juliet I think I have seen the part as well acted as I am likely to.

9. There was a grand baloon ascension which landed in West Wareham.

10. Last Saturday evening we celebrated the first annual existance of our paper amid the enthusiasm of hundreds of people.

11. Probably there was never known such a gathering in town since its foundation, and the result of an establishment of a newspaper in town with such a widespread circulation shows fairly what and who pursues its columns.

12. He was one whom nature seemed to have first made generously and then to have added music as a dominant power.

13. A feeling of sympathy for his fellow man, although in bondage, has at last induced the faculty to put into execution the long-dreamt of idea of laying board-walks throughout the college yard.

14. Some of this wax Ulysses gave to each sailor to put in his ears and prevent him hearing the Sirens.

15. One finds in the reviews of to-day, articles ranging from a sermon to a story and of course many excellent ones, but the efficacy of these latter are destroyed by the stiff, unfamiliar style in which they are written and which usually does away with whatever interest we may take in the subject.

16. We wish to congratulate '87 on her well-earned success, as by winning this race she placed the victor's wreath on her head which will be remembered long after the members of the present seniors are scattered in the four corners of the world.

17. Soliciting your inquiry either in person or letter before you shall locate your home at this Island in the Ocean.

I am, Most Respectfully,

June, 1887.

X. Y.

VIII.

1. The novel itself, as most all of Sir Walter Scott's are, is especially interesting.

2. After a time, she with her Aunt and a guide and Quentin are sent away to a castle.

3. In the purity of his life and actions, as well as in the sheer force of character, he is unequalled by none.

4. One of the strangers, having been informed of the youth's mission set out to find the sought for uncle of the youth.

5. A woman who voted differently than her husband did would be an exception.

6. I have no reference to cooks, servant girls, and senator's wives all elbowing each other in line.

7. As the book goes on Dickens began to see the strong and good points in his people's characters and to unconsciously pass over their weak points.

8. They were given tickets for next time, shoved out of the door, and the stray hats thrown after them.

9. New strata is laid down on the sea floor much more quickly than on land.

10. Everything should be done by not only the college men but also by the faculty.

11. If the tariff were taken off of wool, we would be obliged to close our mills on account of foreign competition.

12. All that they could see of the invisible one were his boots.

13. It prevents him bending the elbow more than a little ways.

14. Brandy sets in motion the functions of the body that fatigue or emotion have paralyzed.

15. Turning into the Square, the post hit him causing him to shy.

June, 1888.

IX.

1. A few years later he began his "Paradise Regained," but which he never finished.

2. While sitting in my room just after lunch, the fire alarm sounded.

3. The character of the agents, or persons, are next to be considered.

4. So honorable a connection might have been expected to have advanced our author's prospects.

5. Sometimes he would lay awake the whole night, trying but unable to make a single line.

6. Milton was too busy to much miss his wife.

7. Everybody had in their recollection the originals of the passages parodied.

8. Dryden neither became Master of Arts or a fellow of the University.

9. He consoles himself with the fancy that he had done a great work.

10. I think we will fall considerably under the mark in computing the poet's income at £600.

11. The Faculty from virtue of its position know thoroughly the needs of the students under them.

12. She confessed to having struck her husband with the axe, and plead self defence.

June, 1889.

X.

1. Would not Shakspere have been likely to at least have heard of these savages?

2. Neither he nor his father were educated to be lawyers.

3. While at Brussels a duel was fought between Thompson and a Russian with whom he had been travelling and suspected of slandering him.

4. He sent me a verbal message and which assured me of the truth of my suspicions.

5. He claimed that Smith, whom he supposed was an American, had written him a letter.

6. I suppose that the purpose of inaugurating those games were the promotion of physical culture.

7. I never have and I hope I never will see him.

8. Did England have the right to levy the Stamp Act?

9. I think I will be able to pay you within a week, for I am liable to receive $500 from my father any day.

10. Cæsar assailed him vigorously, to which he replied, and neither of them were sparing of insults on the other.

11. I do not know but what I'd ought to have been clearer.

12. The United States are not bound to a treaty entered upon without its authority.

June, 1890.

XI.

1. There was little doubt but what she was poisoned, but nobody knew where it was bought.

2. At Rugby each game has its appointed season. Foot-ball reaches its height during the Christmas term, but during the warm weather its place is usurped by hare-and-hounds.

3. The student is enabled to choose his studies from a broad field, thereby allowing him to make proper distinctions in his choice.

4. Molière's plot and idea is often taken from other writers, which he does not attempt to deny.

5. By the constitution of the United States a legislative, executive, and judicial department is established. The legislative department consists in two houses. The members of the lower house are elected by popular suffrage and the number of representatives are apportioned among the several states according to their population.

6. He believed in making the states one in regard to foreign affairs, but that in regard to petty matters each state was to completely control its own administration.

7. Troop A, the cavalry of the force, was only organized a few years ago. It is as well equipped as if it was a part of the regular army.

8. If you are home this afternoon I would be happy to call.

9. He has now been three years in the ministry and is very pleased with that avocation.

10. I had never been in the house but a few times and I hardly felt well acquainted with either of the three members of Mr. Thomas' family.

11. The canvassing the county was quite difficult, but when Mr. Courtney had once gotten the voter's pledges he felt easy.

June, 1891.

XII.

1. Immediately every-body went to sleep just as they were.

2. The 10th regiment were not directed to even attack; yet they remained all night at the station under a severe fire, but which they lost less men from than any regiment there.

3. The fairies promised that their daughter would not die, but would sleep for a hundred years, and that the whole court would fall asleep at the same time.

4. Discussing this subject with a friend, he told me that to clearly understand the relation I must read the books.

5. The prince asked her for most every dance.

6. He would neither buy a coat or a hat.

7. He said that he would give it to either of us—you or John or I.

8. I confess that I thought that he would try and get the bill passed.

9. She said that she had lain the book on the table.

10. It seems to me that by making a great effort to hold your attention on the speaker, and then jot down the things you consider most important, that in course of time and by constant practice one can finally begin to take valuable notes.

11. I studied Latin some when I was home.

12. We will be liable to have a pleasant evening at Miss Jones'.

13. Be sure to behave yourself.

June, 1892.

XIII.

1. While bemoaning the loss of his hound whom he thought was mortally wounded, and the loss of his honor, the physician came up to him and tried to console him.

2. After explaining to Sir Kenneth the reason he is travelling so far from his native city, he opens a satchel and taking out a small bottle he gives a dose of it to the king.

3. He would allow no one to open their eyes while at prayers, and would of times raise up and look around him to see if all were praying.

4. Kenneth was treated and cared for in the most luxuriant manner and his dog was healed.

5. Duty called him in two directions. Which was he to obey?

6. His servants were the ones to feel the most affection for him, his death very near broke their hearts.

7. He refused, knowing that if anything should happen to the banner he would be responsible.

8. Darkness soon spread like a mantel over the spot. He now determined to go to the tent of Berengaria where Edith was stopping.

9. The inquiry was always understood as a rebuke, to the absent one, while Sir Roger did not hesitate to publicly reprimand anyone who he thought deserved his censure.

10. When the curtain finally dropped for the last time, he was greatly moved by the tragical end & could not overcome his feeling for quiet a time.

11. They were encamped not far from the Desert of "Sahara, and King Richard was seized with one of those slow and lasting fevers, which are peculiar to Asia, while encamped at this place.

12. Sir Kenneth hastened to the mound and found his dog laying on his side with a spear-head protruding. The banner was gone.

13. The message demanded him to leave his post.

14. Quickly he drew out his sword and prepared to attack the man whom he supposed was an enemy.

15. Kenneth dimly espied in the morning gloom a small dwarf which he recognized as the one he had seen at the hermit's chapel a few days before.

September, 1892.

MASSACHUSETTS INSTITUTE OF TECHNOLOGY.

I.

1. He would have laid there till now if we hadn't helped him up.

2. Can I have the key to your room. Or will I ask the janitor for it?

3. If he hadn't given me a ride, I never would have been there in time.

4. If it don't come before five, I shall have to go for it myself.

5. Have either of you a copy of this morning's herald.

6. It is just as good, if not better, than any other brand in the market.

7. I have no doubt but what he meant to have told you so long ago.

8. Every intelligent student ought to use their influence in behalf of such a scheme.

9. The old method is quite different in character than that now in use.

10. He knew, as even a boy younger than him would have known, that he was only admitted on certain conditions.

11. The fact of the case was this, when a boy he had been a shirk. When a man, a coward.

12. He was disappointed to lose such a good bargain in the flour line.

13. Freeing himself with a great effort, the blow was warded off, and Harold escaped unharmed.

14. We are very careful who we let in the club, for we want to keep it very select.

15. The signs of the times whose meaning could not possibly be mistaken showed that Lincoln would be elected.

June, 1890.

II.

1. No professional man, no business man, in fact no man of sense would risk their reputations by supporting such a scheme.

2. If it wasn't for the newspapers, we would know very little of what is going on around us.

3. Every one who read that series of brilliant stories was anxious to know whom the writer could have been.

4. To enthuse over the fact that an amateur walkist, our countryman, has beaten the world's record is, so to speak, the duty of every patriotic citizen.

5. Which of you boys left your book laying on the desk.

6. Language of that sort, profane and illiterate, and which I am ashamed to repeat, could have been used only by a member of a very low strata of society.

7. You call his conduct quite aggravating. It is more than that: it is very aggravating.

8. Most of my gramatical knowledge of english has been derived from exercises in parceing.

9. For fifty miles the river could only be distinguished from the ocean by its calmness and discolored water.

10. I have now traveled through nearly every department in France and I do not remember ever meeting with a dirty bed· this, I fear, cannot be said of our happily in all other respects cleaner island.

11. I am now in an unpleasant dilemma: will I takc rooms in Mrs. Brown's boarding-house or shall I live at home?

12. The enormous expense of governments based upon the divine right, as well as upon the greed and avarice, of kings, have provoked men to think by making them feel.

13. Every one of the witnesses gave it as their opinion that neither the captain nor the mate were in any way responsible for the disaster.

14. Much as I had hoped to have seen him he don't seem to in the least regret missing me.

15. Being exceedingly fond of birds an aviary is always to be found on his grounds.

September, 1890.

III.

1. He has sent all three of his servents though heaven knows that either of them would do the errand plenty well enough.

2. A general as brave as he and who is known throughout the country as a man of honor should not have been concerned in such a disgraceful affair.

3. When I wrote you, I expected to have met him that afternoon.

4. Neither pupil nor teacher are able to accomplish their proper work under such adverse circumstances.

5. No nation but ourselves have equally succeeded in both forms of the higher poetry epic and tragic.

6. At least I am resolved that the country shall know who it has to thank for whatever may happen.

7. The then monarchies are strongly in contrast with the now governments, democratic or otherwise.

8. A more startling phenomena than this upturned strata has never been observed in geology's whole history.

9. With some difficulty he fished up the gun which was laying on the bottom of the pool. Will I carry it home now, he asked himself, or will I leave it until John comes with the team.

10. [*Punctuate the following passage, using capital letters when they are needed.*]

for the first time in the history of christianity rome was deserted by the popes the city which held such power over the minds of men as the capital of the civilized world though its glory had departed and its magnificence was buried deep in the dust of the middle ages was for a time no longer to be the abode of the supreme pontiff with the close of the short pontificate of the calm and wise benedict the babylonish captivity as it is so often called began and for more than seventy years no successor of st peter was to sit on the throne of st peter.

June, 1891.

IV.

1. The vote of the corporation on the resolution sustaining Mr. Smith was six in the affirmative, four in the negative, with one member absent whom it is claimed by the opposition would have voted in the negative.

2. Neither his father nor he were willing to have anything to do with a man who treated them so shamefully.

3. I only said I wouldn't go without he promised to pay all my expenses for the entire trip.

4. The death of Gen. Grant transpired during 1885, that was a year remarkable for many deaths among prominent Americans.

5. But if I do not review algebra now I will forget the greater part of it before the September examinations, having so much other work to do.

6. The German public evidently has a different notion of what a good novel is than that which we have in America.

7. It is not to much to say that he is known most and best by a single story, famous in France and Italy, and which even in America we have not had time to quite forget.

8. It is most efficacious when taken fasting and mixed with an equal quantity of water.

9. Sometimes he would lay awake a whole night, full of enthusiasm for these sort of poems, but unable to write a line of poetry for himself.

10. Nearly every one of the teachers present gave it as their opinion that there was more than one way of answering the question, and that consequently neither of the three answers were absolutely wrong.

Punctuate the following passage, using capitals wherever they are necessary: —

it was amidst these noble recollections this solemn nature and upon that predestinated height that the patriarch of the monks of the west founded the capital of the monastic order he found paganism still surviving there two hundred years after constantine in the heart of christendom and so near rome there still existed a very ancient temple of apollo and a sacred wood where a multitude of peasants sacrificed to the gods and demons benedict preached the faith of christ to these forgotten people he persuaded them to cut down the wood to overthrow the temple and the idol

September, 1891.

V.

Punctuate (on this paper) the following passage, using capitals whenever they are necessary:—

the place was worthy of such a trial, it was the great hall of william rufus, the hall which had resounded with acclamations at the inauguration of thirty kings the hall which had witnessed the just sentence of bacon and the just absolution of somers, the hall where the eloquence of strafford had for a moment awed and melted a victorious party inflamed with just resentment, the hall where charles had confronted the high court of justice with the placid courage which has half redeemed his fame, neither military nor civil pomp was wanting, the avenues were lined with grenadiers, the streets were kept clear by cavalry, the peers robed in gold and ermine, were marshalled by heralds under garter king-at-arms, the judges in their vestments of state attended to give advice on points of law, the gray old walls were hung with scarlet, the long galleries were crowded by an audience such as has rarely excited the fears or the emulation of an orator, there were gathered together from all parts of a great free enlightened and prosperous empire grace and female loveliness wit and learning, the representatives of every science and of every art, there were seated round the queen the fair-haired young daughters of the house of brunswick.

Correct on the margin of this paper all the errors you discover in the following sentences:—

1. The rain came down and continued during the time the cyclists had their competition, clearing off about half-past twelve, and continuing fine the remainder of the day.

2. My bachelor friend settles himself comfortably in an arm-chair, gives my companion a mock-heroic glance, closed his eyes, but never for one moment paused from caressing his moustache.

3. The present member and myself will have the pleasure of holding meetings in the various parts of the division, where we will be able more fully to express our views, and be ready and willing to answer any questions, and trust thereby to secure your votes and interests.

4. I am a man who approves of wholesome discipline, and who recommend it to others; but I am not a person who promotes severity, or who object to mild and generous treatment.

5. The prince or magistrate, the soldier or merchant, reconciled their fervent zeal and implicit faith with the exercise of their profession, the pursuit of their interest, and the indulgence of their passions.

6. This was as far as he could carry the case that day, as a witness whom he expected would have been present was unfortunately absent.

7. Mr. Walter Smith, who, it is announced, the president has appointed American minister to Russia, is a distinguished journalist.

8. I neither attempted to conceal from myself nor from him that the enterprise would be a dangerous one.

June, 1892.

Punctuate (on this paper) the following passage, using capitals whenever they are necessary:—

byron has told us himself that the giaour is but a string of passages he has made full confession of his own negligence no one says he has done more through negligence to corrupt the language this accusation brought by himself against his poems is not just but when he goes on to say of them that their faults whatever they may be are those of negligence and not of labor he says what is perfectly true lara he declares I wrote while undressing after coming home from balls and masquerades in the year of revelry 1814 the bride was written in four the corsair in ten days he calls this a humiliating confession as it proves my own want of judgment in publishing and the publics in reading things which cannot have stamina for permanence again he does his poems injustice the producer of such poems could not but publish them the public could not but read them nor could byron have produced his work in any other fashion his poetic work could not have first grown and matured in his own mind and then come forth as an organic whole byron had not enough of the artist in him for this nor enough of self-command.

Specimens of Bad English.

1. It is decided that if the weather is favorable we will sail to-morrow, but that if to-morrow is stormy not only will we wait fair weather but for the hop Thursday night.

2. Having made careful preparations there was no delay; the band strikes up a favorite air, the driver of the first van cracks his whip, and the parade begins.

3. The crowd, numbering about 4100, one third of which were ladies, were delighted with the game and applauded vigorously.

4. It is said that many a one has gone out of the world no wiser than when they came into it; yet the meaning of historical events, for instance, can be made clear to very young pupils, and should have a lasting effect upon their mind and life.

5. Their conduct was more like a wild Indians than civilized people; what will we do with them?

6. Distributing the oranges between the nine ragged little fellows, I tried to reconcile them with the loss of their play-ground.

September, 1892.

CPSIA information can be obtained at www.ICGtesting.com
Printed in the USA
LVOW10s1021310816

502638LV00022B/487/P

9 781330 506042